CW00336461

STEEP HOLM
ALLSOP ISLAND

RODNEY LEGG tells the story of
the adventures of **JOHN FOWLES**
and friends in buying an 'inaccessible'
offshore island as a tribute to
television anchor-man **KENNETH ALLSOP**

Wincanton Press
National School, North Street, Wincanton, Somerset BA9 9AT

Publishing details. First published 1992. Copyright © Rodney Legg 1992
Provisional permission for copying. This is intended as a source book for information
on Steep Holm and material may be quoted from it, providing the source is
acknowledged and mention is made of the work of the Kenneth Allsop Memorial Trust
in conserving the island. All other rights are reserved.
Printing credits. Typesetting input by Reg Ward at Holwell, Dorset, and output by
Wordstream Limited, Poole.
Illustrations processed by Flaydemouse [sic, third version of their (mis)spelling] Printing
Studio, 8 Buckland Road, Yeovil, Somerset.
Printed in Wiltshire by the Fairwood Press at Dilton Marsh, Westbury. Telephone 0373
822044
Distribution. By Dorset Publishing Company from the Wincanton Press, National
School, North Street, Wincanton, Somerset BA9 9AT. Telephone 0963 32583.
International Standard Book Number. ISBN 0 948699 61 2.

For **Zilli Sternfeld**
and her **John Fowles** collection

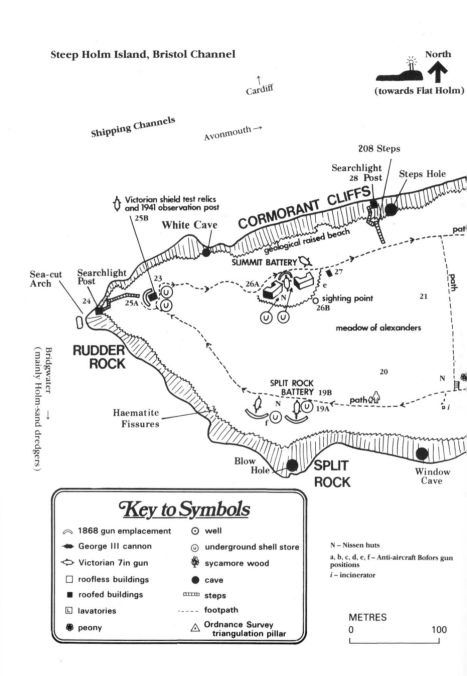

Steep Holm Island, Bristol Channel

North

(towards Flat Holm)

↑ Cardiff

Shipping Channels

Avonmouth →

208 Steps

Searchlight
28 Post

Steps Hole

Victorian shield test relics
and 1941 observation post
25B

White Cave

CORMORANT CLIFFS

path

geological raised beach

SUMMIT BATTERY

Sea-cut
Arch

Searchlight
Post

23

27
e

path

24

25A

26A

21

N

sighting point
26B

RUDDER
ROCK

meadow of alexanders

20

N

Bridgwater
(mainly Holm-sand dredgers)

Haematite
Fissures

SPLIT ROCK
BATTERY   19B

path

N

f

19A

i

Blow
Hole

SPLIT
ROCK

Window
Cave

Key to Symbols

⌒ 1868 gun emplacement   ⊙ well
➤ George III cannon   Ⓤ underground shell store   N – Nissen huts
⬦ Victorian 7in gun   🌳 sycamore wood   a, b, c, d, e, f – Anti-aircraft Bofors gun
☐ roofless buildings   ● cave   positions
■ roofed buildings   ⊞⊞⊞ steps   i – incinerator
Ⓛ lavatories   - - - - footpath
🌺 peony   △ Ordnance Survey
                                    triangulation pillar

METRES
0   100

Rodney Legg has written other books on the nature reserve island of Steep Holm in the Bristol Channel:

THE STEEP HOLM GUIDE (1985, ISBN 0'902129 62 7)
STEEP HOLM WILDLIFE (1990, with Tony Parsons, ISBN 0 948699 59 0)
ISLAND CAT (1991, ISBN 0 0948699 27 2)
STEEP HOLM AT WAR (1991, ISBN 0 948699 60 4)
STEEP HOLM LEGENDS AND HISTORY (1992, ISBN 0 948699 60 4)

Map: of the island of Steep Holm, which lies in the middle of the Bristol Channel, six miles west of Weston-super-Mare, England, and seven miles south-east of Penarth, Wales. Drawn by Malcolm Noyes in 1978 and revised by Rodney Legg in 1990.

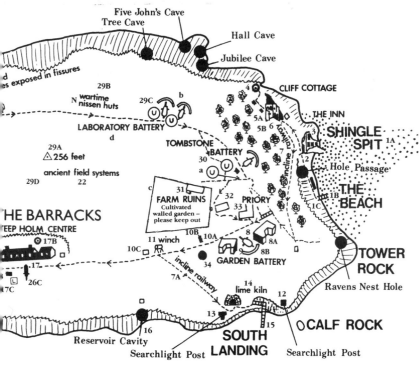

Map numbers

1A	Stakes for nets	10C	Generator house	24	Searchlight post
1B	Beach landing	11	Railway winch	25A	Rudder Rock Battery
1C	Bristol boundary stone	12	Searchlight post	25B	Battery Observation Post
2	Telephone exchange	13	Searchlight post	26A	Coast Defence Battery
3	Inn/Warden's depot	14	Limekiln	26B	Coast Defence Battery
4	Monks' well)	15	Jetty	26C	Georgian cannon
5	Cliff or Smugglers Cottage	16	Water-haul	27	Generator house
5A	Water tank bases	17	Steep Holm Centre/Barracks	28	Searchlight post
6	Allsop plaque	17B	Water tank	29A	Triangulation pillar
7	East cliff railway	17C	Latrines	29B	Latrines
7A	South Landing railway	18	Boundary stone	29C	Laboratory Battery
8	Garden Battery)	19A	Split Rock Battery	29D	Water & fuel tank bases
8A	Coast Defence Battery	19B	Latrines	30	Tombstone Battery
8B	Range-finding point	20	Cultivation terraces	31	Farmstead/"Garden Cottage"
9	Coast Defence Battery	21	Field boundaries	32	Tenement ruin
10A	Generator house	22	Field boundaries	33	St Michael's Priory
10B	Limekiln	23	Boundary stones	34	Parsons Cave

Football: professional foul as Salman Legg kicks a rock-hard Herring Gull egg from a nest beneath the 24-pounder cannon military display-piece outside the Barracks on Steep Holm. The egg was already abandoned as the birds were unable to cope with disturbance from two-legged visitors. Seen from the north. Photographed by Rodney Legg in 1991.

Introduction

to the Steep Holm Trilogy:
the first book is *Steep Holm Legends and History*,
and the second *Steep Holm at War*

You can find Britain in microcosm on an offshore island. That has to be the justification for inflicting more than a quarter of a million words on what is barely fifty acres of rock. Thomas Hardy, who had less need of excuses, felt it better to know a small area exceedingly well than the whole world a little.

Steep Holm is poised on the horizon between England and Wales, half-way between Weston-super-Mare and Cardiff at latitude 51 degrees 20½ minutes north, longitude 3 degrees 6½ minutes west; the next place in the latter direction is Goose Cove, Newfoundland. The island has been touched by events from both sides of the Bristol Channel. Occupants have included the Romans, the Danes, the Christians, the Coast Guard and the Royal Artillery.

None found it tractable. This is nature's environment. Botanical explorers may come on tropical days and find their flowers but otherwise the island maintains hostility to man. It performs better when left to the seabirds but even they never find peace.

I have been asked to point out that the views expressed, particularly in this book, are often my own rather than those of the Allsop Trust's current council. My response is that this is an investigation into contemporary history and the opinions belong where they are attributed. Many were indeed those of the Trust as an organisation, or its officers, at the time they were expressed. Subsequent adjustment and revision is not, fortunately, a problem for the historian. As L.P. Hartley writes in *The Go-Between*: "The past is another country, they do things differently there."

Truth, I feel upon a reminder from Michael Yardley, is the only god an historian serves – though how well is open to doubt as I have deleted three substantial references in the face of sensitivity from others.

I have not, however, agreed to the removal of the quotations from "private correspondence never intended for publication" as none of it was secret at the time. With few exceptions, and those where quoted here are hurtful to me rather than to others, such extracts have been read to meetings of the Kenneth Allsop Memorial Trust or otherwise reported to its officers and in some cases even circulated to the press. "This could destroy all faith in your integrity," I have been told. If so, I shall be the loser, but what you have here endeavours to meet a dictionary definition of the word – "being entire or complete; entireness; a genuine or unimpaired state; honesty; uprightness in mutual dealings; probity". I am many things, but not a hypocrite.

Since 1974 it has been my weekend task to warden Steep Holm in its late twentieth century rôle as a nature reserve. Inherently and strategically it is an exceedingly important sanctuary and it is run as a tight ship along a course charted by the ideals and aspirations of the naturalist and broadcaster Kenneth Allsop.

A ferry to the island runs out of Knightstone Causeway, Weston-super-Mare, either an hour and a half before high-tide or a similar time after the water has turned, on most Saturdays and Bank Holiday Mondays from April to October. Booking details can be had from the Tourist Information Office at Beach Lawns on Weston seafront. The island, as will become clear in this book, is primarily cherished as wilderness, but there is also a place for humans. "Holm" was the Viking word for an estuary island. If at times its name is rendered "Steepe Holmes" in Victorian fashion, or any other variation in spelling, I have left such inconsistencies because we tolerate idiosyncracies on this island.

Here I escape the word factory, from research as an historian and incarcerations at the typewriter, and sail back to permanent adolescence. Steep Holm has been a tithe on my life, its resources, and my writings. I hope that at times the spirit of the island will break through the verbiage and give you momentary flashes of the impetuous fury of romantic attachment.

R.L.
The Barracks, Steep Holm
County of Avon (detached)
1 iv 91

OPPOSITE:
Words flowed: Kenneth Allsop [1920-73] beside the water of his Milton Mill home in the hills north-east of Bridport, Dorset. Photographed for one of his many features which became the book 'In the Country' in 1972.

REMEMBERING
HARRY COX
CUSTODIAN OF THE
BIRDS AND FLOWERS
OF
STEEP HOLM
1930 – 1949

Birdwatchers: plaque on a Second World War Royal Artillery range-finding station at Garden Battery, for island warden Harry Cox. Salman Legg takes a professional interest in the wildlife; Cox also blotted his copy book, trying to gas badgers on Brean Down. Seen from the north. Photographed by Rodney Legg in 1991.

Baron Wharton's Island

Steep Holm had already been set aside for the birds before the Second World War. In 1930 the Wharton family leased Steep Holm to Harry Cox, an unpaid warden for the Royal Society for the Protection of Birds, who looked after the nature reserve on Brean Down. There he once tried to gas the badgers in a misguided effort to placate grumbling farmers. After Cox died, in 1949, his executors retained the island lease and allowed a few visiting parties of naturalists to use the island. It was again regarded as a wildlife sanctuary, but doubts about its future were beginning to arise.

Baron Wharton's land in the West Country was "settled" as a family trust, with the London bankers Arthur and Edward Hoare appointed as trustees. Lord Wharton remained Steep Holm's tenant-for-life and in 1953 he firmly committed himself to the cause of conservation and rented the island to Harry Savory, Marie Colthurst, Edmund Mason and Eric Kelting – representing an amalgam of the Bristol Naturalists' Society, the Somerset Archaeological and Natural History Society, Folk House Archaeological Club and the Mid-Somerset Naturalists' Society. They paid £26 a year. Conditions were imposed. The island had to be preserved "as a sanctuary for birds and wildlife" and "nothing shall be done to damage the old emplacements and cannon". Archaeological finds had to be reported within fourteen days of their discovery and the tenants were required to "prepare and keep a catalogue of all such finds" which would "belong to and remain vested in the landlord". All the usual farming conditions and terms had now disappeared from the Steep Holm lease and the groups' involvement in the island was for "ecological and archaeological research" as well as education purposes. It was a comprehensive document and it opened the way for diversified studies, although these tended to centre on the Priory and the gulls.

Harry Savory died in 1962. Earlier in that year he had "cleared an appreciable amount of privet and sycamore from the Peony glens" and it was due to his efforts that the Peony survived in the changing ecology of the late 1950s. The results of his work were splendidly rewarded in the year he died. "The glens have produced the most magnificent display of blooms known for a very long time."

The final Baron Wharton – Charles John Halswell Kemeys-Tynte – was born on 12 January 1908 and died "without issue" at Mougins in the Alpes Maritimes, France, on 11 July 1969. His home had been in Lausanne, Switzerland. He directed in his will that his heart should be removed from his body and the corpse placed in a coffin to which "no lid is to be fitted". It was then cremated, and his ashes scattered or interred somewhere in England "other than at my family burial place in the county of Somerset" (the chapel at Halswell Park) without mourning or flowers. His principal beneficiary was Major Malcolm Ludovic Munthe, MC, of the Norwegian family of landscape painters. The Wharton line had ended.

After Lord Wharton's death, control of the island was held by Dorothy, Baroness Wharton. She was a veterinary surgeon living in Portugal and her principal interest in the island was also the survival of the Wild Peony. She worried about excavations that had taken place at the Priory and decided she could only sell Steep Holm to an organisation capable of safeguarding the island's natural history. Tentative approaches were made to the existing island trust but no appeal was launched to raise money for the freehold. The National Trust, feeling the burden of its massive influx of coastal holdings that had resulted from Enterprise Neptune, was also approached but declined.

The achievement of the Steep Holm Trust's era was the scientific work carried out by Ray Poulding from Bristol. He had been visiting the island since "several observers organised expeditions in 1949, covering in all a period of thirteen days". That, he thought, was the longest period to date that the birds of Steep Holm had been studied.

He would go on to put Steep Holm into the pioneering vanguard of bird research with work, carried out in 1963, that showed for the first time how Dunnocks could be aged from their changing iris colour. This sequence is now in general use by ringers. The work was made possible by the island's resident population of some forty pairs being a closed one, independent of the mainland.

Poulding also established the Gull Research Station in the island's Barracks. He saw the possibilities for using extruded plastics to mark the larger birds and was the first to send coloured tags into the sky on his gulls.

An attractive proposition for bird people was that a distinctive "Steep Holm Wren" might have developed. Colin Graham suggested it when we first explored the island, in 1974, but Dennis Lovell had raised the possibility long before that, in the Agricultural Magazine for July-August 1952, where after mentioning his sighting of a Wren he adds: "It occurred to me that the latter might be a new sub-species, akin to the St Kilda Wren, for I

10

carefully noted that its bill was bigger and its tail more erect than those of the mainland kind."

I doubt if Poulding thought there was anything in the idea, and our ornithologist, Tony Parsons, was quick to dismiss the notion. "The wren is usually a sedentary species and will undoubtedly repay studying in detail," he agreed, but though some observers had "claimed plumage variations in comparison with mainland birds" he considered "much work would be necessary to determine any consistent variation and it is unlikely that a distinctive 'Steep Holm Wren' is ever going to arise".

A cat was going to have the last word on the subject. There were well over a hundred Wrens as the post-breeding population on the island in 1976, and this high level only gradually tailed off. Many were netted by Tony Parsons. Colin Graham and I imagined that they were all-year residents and that at most only odd ones drifted across to the mainland. The ring that came back from the cat-caught specimen showed a considerable flight for a "sedentary species". The kill had been made in a Paris street; not quite the evidence that convinces people about an island sub-species.

I hope that Ray Poulding enjoys this story, and that he has approved of the retrospective association of Steep Holm with another of Britain's most devoted twentieth century bird-men.

Kenneth Allsop

Kenneth Allsop [1920-73] came into my life long before I had ever heard of Steep Holm. As I lay on the floor doing my homework in the early 1960s his was one of the most familiar voices from above, on the telly. With deceptive softness in both tone and looks, he did intense studio interviews for the "Tonight" news magazine. He was still as engagingly youthful, as instantly recognisable by both sight and sound to just about every person in the country, when he came down to Dorset from Hertfordshire, in 1970.

I knew who it was on the telephone before he gave the magic name. That was a call about oilmen exploring in the deep-cut valleys around his mill-house home at West Milton, near Bridport. I was the editor of Dorset County Magazine, which I had founded in 1968, and was the nearest thing Dorset then had, or has since had, to an investigative environmental journalist. Ken's enthusiasm and application to this and other countryside causes was constant and total. The phone calls were often from studios of the BBC in London, where he was the linkman for "24 Hours" and "Down to Earth". The conversations would take up most of the time when, had he been anyone else, he would have been preparing the programme. He would break off at last with the words: "I must go, they are waving for me to come through."

Five minutes later and he would be on air and once again in our living room. Not that I can claim to have been his friend. I did not so much know the man as share his obsessions. We had skipped the opportunity for friendship and moved into something that was deeper; what motivated Ken Allsop was a commitment to wildlife and ecology that had the vision and the passion that a minority of others reserve for their religion.

It was as dangerous and destructive as a holy war. His handsome appearance and mental agility were not matched by the physical reality of the body behind the television mask. This had been mangled in an assault training course in 1943, falling over hurdles whilst in the Royal Air Force, and his hospitalisation continued until the end of the war when he finally insisted that they amputate his leg. Taking painkillers was a matter of routine but he would never show this agony, even when he forced himself to keep up with us as we went on a site visit through the impenetrable boglands of Powerstock Common. Neither, on principle, would he accept a helping hand.

He was an implacable opponent. When he had the opposition in front of him even in the hospitable neutral ground of a public house, he did not lapse for a moment into the diplomatic pleasantries that normally accompany a drink. "You hate me, don't you!" the official from the Forestry Commission exploded. Ken had won. He didn't even deny it, to the embarrassment of the rest of us who struggled to maintain the social conventions. Kenneth used the power that was his, not through any position, or as a national newspaper columnist, broadcaster and author of many books, but that existed through sheer force of intellect and personality.

He was workaholic. I have never shivered naked at the telephone for longer than I regularly used to, at both ends of the day, after Kenneth had phoned once again. There was no escape. "You have to keep writing when the words are flowing," he wrote at two a.m. as the typewriter rippled to the accompaniment of his mill-race.

Which leads me to our last conversation. It was in the morning of 22 May 1973 that he phoned, chirpy and the absolute epitome of charm. What was unusual was the content and the instructions, down to the dictation of a letter, to be sent in by proxy, complaining about an omission which had been edited out in his article about the Tyneham tank gunnery ranges in the current issue of the Sunday Times. He went on for an hour and a quarter spelling out just what he felt about this issue and that, and was probably ticking off a list as he went, and interspersed superfluous apologies for things that had not been done or might be taken wrongly.

The following morning was wet, with low clouds settling into the west Dorset valleys, and Betty, his wife, had taken their daughter, Amanda, to London for her birthday. It was then that Ken took an overdose of painkillers. There would be an open verdict at the inquest but I was later shown some of his final text that had been hand-written after my telephone call. The moving and tragic description of his final decision was broadcast in 1990, in the programme "Letters from my Father". In it he enthused about the exhilaration of his magical day in Pembroke-shire on 20 May, when he saw Peregrine stoops, but also ago-nised on paper – as he had to me in the call – that man, the species, was the ugly predator killing this planet.

He had had enough of us. "I've a deadline to keep," was the last awful pun of his life. He could never quite control the purple prose.

John Fowles, the author of *The French Lieutenant's Woman* and *The Magus*, who also lived in Dorset, at Lyme Regis, was in France at the time:

"Something strange happened to me on the day of Kenneth Allsop's death. I was driving round France with my wife, and about three o'clock that afternoon we stopped in the little town of La Rochefoucauld to look at the famous chateau there. But as we crossed the bridge over the river that runs in front of it, something caught my eye.

"It was a swift, hanging suspended from some high tele-phone wires over the water. There were boys fishing and the bird must have taken a fly off the end of one of their lines. The hook was in its gullet, the gut somehow wrapped round the wires. There was absolutely no way to rescue it. Repeatedly the poor creature flapped, winnowed a frantic foot or two up, then fell again and was jerked to a stop.

"Out of nowhere the thought of Ken drifted into my mind: how I would have to tell him about this when we returned home, how he was one person who would feel the same acute distress that we did. A week later, in another part of France, I picked up an English newspaper and for the first time learnt that at that precise hour of that same May day during which I had watched the swift in its last lonely agony, Ken had also been dying in his Dorset mill.

"In one way it was his misfortune to be so well-known on the television screen, since that side of his career came to overshadow an aspect of his life that was much closer to his heart. Ken didn't merely observe nature, he felt it – felt it with empathetic passion and also, in his last years, with a mounting despair at man's selfishness and greed. At least part of the despair was a by-product of his countless public battles for good conservation causes; in the end he was becoming a sort of unofficial ombudsman in this field. From all over Britain, anyone with an environmental problem tried to enlist his support."

EX LIBRIS

KENNETH ALLSOP

Environmental saviour: Kenneth Allsop's dulcet tones had a deceptively sharp edge that created mayhem for oil-men drilling into the west Dorset countryside – and then foiled Forestry Commission plans for clear-felling primaeval oak woodland on Powerstock Common. Photographed by Colin Graham, at Milton Mill, in 1971.

'Avon (Detached)'

Steep Holm was at this time out of the news. Its only public mention of 1973-74 was a consequence of the local government boundary changes that were overturning a thousand years of history. Despite the use of the island to fix the limits of Bristol's port, there is no part of Steep Holm above the high-tide that has ever had any administrative attachment to the city. The island was always a detached piece of the historic county of Somerset but never part of any parish. It is marked "Somerset (Detached)" on older Ordnance Survey maps and on 1 April 1974, along with the mainland at Weston-super-Mare, it was transferred to the new county of Avon, and has since appeared on the official maps as "Avon (Detached)".

The changes of the 1970s did not bring the island into any parish, and it is worth repeating this fact, as a number of documents and accounts erroneously put it into one mainland parish or another. Lawyers find it difficult to envisage a place that is extraparochial and feel compelled to attach it to somewhere. The mistake even applied to the title-deed to Steep Holm that was drawn up when it was purchased by the Kenneth Allsop Memorial Trust.

It does, however, come inside the area of Woodspring District Council, and for Parliamentary purposes the island is included in the Weston-super-Mare county constituency. No one is listed on its electoral roll. When it last had resident voters the island was part of the Wells division which then stretched from the Somerset seaboard to Dorset. One imagines that if it had residents again there would be a requirement to attend a polling booth in some Weston school, but the system is not so inflexible in the Scottish islands, and the returning officer might relish the thought of a helicopter ride.

Allsop Island

It was six months before Steep Holm made its move from historic Somerset to oblivious Avon that Baroness Wharton's agent, Nigel Murray, who was working in Yeovil, heard of the Kenneth Allsop Memorial Committee and its efforts to create a West Country nature reserve. The committee, formed soon after Kenneth Allsop's death to establish a memorial in his name, negotiated to buy half of Eggardon Hill, a prehistoric fort on a chalkland escarpment near Bridport in Dorset. The owners refused to accept offers below £42,000, then the going rate for prime arable land rather than windswept hilltops, and even the fund's solicitor, Roger House, was prompted to ask – without being aware of the impending pun – "whether the money could not be spent along different channels altogether".

In September 1973 I nearly gave up editing Dorset County Magazine to become the British countryside campaigns organiser for Friends of the Earth. That was an offer I momentarily accepted, confirming to Richard Sandbrook that I would be starting on 29 October, but my partner in the Dorset publishing venture, Colin Graham, insisted that it would cause the collapse of the magazine. One of my prospective colleagues in London wrote me a not-quite "what the hell are you playing at" letter in which he was kind enough to add: "Somebody gets disappointed but that's life."

I would have enjoyed expanding my catalogue of Dorset causes, several of which were Ken-based, into a national collection. On the other hand, working for Richard Sandbrook and Charles Levison would have cramped my style in the little intrigues that were gradually manoeuvring the Allsop Fund into buying the island. Neither, after five days a week campaigning in London, would I have had the energy to turn up on Saturday mornings at Weston seafront. The deciding factor was that I would have missed my tabby cat, Piggy, which in fact I still do every day even now, some years after he was killed.

The pages that follow are autobiographical and at the same time the "kiss and tell" story of how we fell in love with an island and finally bought it against all the odds. I will tell it dispassionately if possible, from the files rather than memory, and at times against myself, because the contemporary history of Steep Holm has moments that make me feel less than admirable.

It was on 19 September 1973 that Nigel Murray phoned me about Steep Holm. "Would you like to consider an island?" he said.

Murray lived at Loscombe, near Bridport, and had written to Betty Allsop on 16 September. His letter is both descriptive and informative. Steep Holm "is leased at present to a private trust and the lease expires in March 1974. The Baroness wishes to sell the island, she thinks to someone, or some group of people who would perpetuate its present use as a bird sanctuary and as an unspoilt site for botanical research. The island is limestone rock and is really an extension of the Mendips which rises up in the Channel. It is the only natural habitat of an exotic Wild Peony in the UK and there is a large gull colony on which a good deal of research is done.

"The island has an interesting history and I could tell you a lot about it but it occurred to me that although not in Dorset it might well be an appropriate memorial to your husband in view of its ornithological interest."

Being offered an island, which I had never even seen from either shore, was a chance of a lifetime but I knew that other committee members of the Kenneth Allsop Memorial Fund had their own pieces of cherished England to offer as alternatives. There could be no assumption of an instant majority in favour of the idea. In fact there could, for a while, be no vote as the outcome would have been to drop Steep Holm as too expensive, with impossibilities of access, and as being a frightening and unending commitment. The idea would have been sunk if anyone had phoned the National Trust regional office for Wessex, at Stourhead, and found that was just what they had concluded. Steep Holm was only going to become a possibility at the cost of splitting the London committee. Several people were going to be hurt.

I had the authority of being almost an honorary Allsop, being engaged to Ken's daughter Amanda who was completing, with just some minor tinkering from me as a professional editor, the compilation of *Letters to his Daughter* for Hamish Hamilton, though I never saw the final proofs, or Mandy's "disinterest" would have been corrected to "uninterest". She was esconced in a separate house in the mill-house grounds. Betty Allsop had not yet sold-up and the weather in the deep-cut trough in the Dorset hills was almost perpetual rain and mist that duplicated the damp morning of Ken's death.

Mandy and I had also fallen in love with the idea of buying Eggardon and had staggered across it in a total hill-fog when the low clouds had the sheep running with globules of water and made the finding of the single windswept hawthorn an achievement to be celebrated by another hug. That emotive tie to Eggardon was loosened only by the likelihood that it was destined to be bought by another conservation agency. It seemed an abuse of publicly-raised money to enter into a virtual auction to buy something that was already earmarked for another composite cheque that would largely be down to HM Paymaster General. In the event it was to be the National Trust that coalesced the successful effort to purchase the southern half of the great Iron Age hill-fort.

Steep Holm was a possibility only because Mandy saw things

the same way and put her intense and bubbling enthusiasm into the alternative. Buying an island, however, did not appeal to those whose minds were still set on Eggardon. Brian Jackman, The Sunday Times environment reporter and the closest of Kenneth Allsop's Dorset friends, pointed out that it was an island that Ken had never even seen – though that applied also to Brian's own second choice, a cowslip meadow in the Thames Valley. Betty Allsop retorted that she, anyway, had looked out on Steep Holm from Penarth. "You would make a good politician," Jackman told me. It was a pity about the cowslips.

Elsewhere we had to be manipulative rather than combative.

John Percival and I started to work on the hearts and minds of other members of the fund-raising committee. Though declining an active part in the more distant future, Andrew Lloyd Webber proved to be Really Useful even then with the vital immediate support of half his share of the proceeds of a charity preview of the film of *Jesus Christ Superstar* in September 1973. He felt, however, that any further personal effort would be better directed towards saving a superb pile of ecclesiastical gothic-revival in, I think, Buckinghamshire, and in which if I recall the sequel he was eventually successful.

Our first boat trip to Steep Holm would have only the rump of the London committee – John Percival, Mandy Allsop and myself – though we had gained two stalwarts from Lyme Regis, John Fowles and his wife and driver Elizabeth. In nervous expectation, and against the fear of another failure, we converged on the Royal Pier Hotel, Weston-super-Mare, on the grey morning of 4 November 1973. John Fowles agreed to give the island his powerful endorsement and our initial impressions were put together as a memo to Betty Allsop:

"There is little evidence of any management work carried out on the island. No attempt has been made even to tidy up loose pieces of wartime ironwork. Members of the present island trust say that doubts about their future have not encouraged much recent work. It was disappointing, however, to find there is no organised volunteer labour force in existence. We heard of friction between archaeologists and gull ringers. The gull researchers had defended their territorial rights as ably as the gulls themselves. They stopped an excavation on the grounds that the dig was disturbing the birds. Obviously the extreme numbers of gulls (and not archaeologists) make the island unattractive for other rock-nesting birds. Though the island has been abandoned to nature since the war it is without noticeable worthwhile results. Rival introduced plants fight for space in the way any once-cultivated land reverts to an accidental type of wilderness far different from its primaeval state. There is no chance of the natural flora recovering as it is now extinct as far as the island is concerned."

John Percival, a television producer who had worked with Kenneth Allsop and had the idea for his environmental programme "Down to Earth", summed it up: "It's the flora of the average British bomb-site with elder, privet and brambles." John Fowles pointed out that an examination of the Brean Down flora on the Somerset coast would provide a list of plants that should have been expected on the island as well. The first essential task for conservationists moving into an unknown piece of land is to prepare lists of all the life that is there initially, but on Steep Holm much of the knowledge was passed on by a form of twentieth century folklore.

Discussion showed that there was great confusion over the plants, birds, insects and mammals different people claimed were present on the island. Despite the contradictions it was an encouraging day: "In every way the island is experiencing an ecological low, yet it has immense potential and could become a place of great beauty again, and attractive to every visitor to Weston-super-Mare."

Both Mr and Mrs Fowles would be notable acquisitions. John Robert Fowles, who had been born on 31 March 1926, was already a cult figure and on his way to becoming one of the leading novelists in the western world. He had a matching physical stature, not unlike Orson Welles, and a Solzhenytzin-style beard. He had married Elizabeth Whitton who was both protective and practical. To call her commonsensical would be wrong, because that is the metaphysics of savages, but she brought a certain worldliness to the relationship. It was spiced with delightful humour. I would one day find two puzzled old ladies waiting expectantly on the beach at Steep Holm for three o'clock because they had heard "from a very cultured lady" that it was the time "the headless sea captain"was set to appear. They were marvellous company to be stranded with overnight, even though John had already shared most of his hip-flask on the top of some crag and did not pick a diplomatic moment to point out that on the South Coast "weather like this often goes on for a week". Mr and Mrs Fowles liked the island and their influence would be vital in turning the proposals into reality.

John Fowles clinched the Allsop family's support for the island when he presented Ken's widow, Betty, with a 'quasi-formal' outline of its three great assets: "Firstly, a breeding sanctuary and resting-place for migrants. Secondly as a site for an experiment, properly controlled, in improving an impoverished, unbalanced and already very 'corrupt' ecology. Thirdly an amenity site – a kind of true wildlife park – for nature-loving human visitors." He suggested organised visiting as the way to finance management of the island: "The atmosphere of the island contrives, because of all the old military paraphernalia, to be both very beautiful and very bizarre, and I see no reason at all why the public, paying a landing fee and kept within reasonable numbers, should be kept away as remorselessly as at present.

"I do hope the plunge is taken," he continued. " For all its inscrutables, such a project seems to me in a way much closer to what Ken stood for than the buying of some piece of already reasonably 'safe' ground (such as Eggardon Hill) because of personal association. To me that would seem a little like a green gravestone. But somehow I think he would still be alive on Steep Holm, purely because it is a challenge, it does need work and energy and people to love it and take it in hand ... and it could be such an exciting and worthwhile venture, both publicly and conservationally."

The crucial meeting that decided the Kenneth Allsop Memorial Fund should negotiate to buy Steep Holm took place in London at the offices of the Friends of the Earth, 9 Poland Street, on 12 November 1973. It was the sixth meeting of the fund's committee. Richard Mabey, who had just published *Food for Free*, joined Amanda Allsop, Brian Jackman, John Percival and myself for a debate on the pros and cons of what had now become a choice between a field in Dorset or an island. Baroness Wharton was prepared to sell Steep Holm for something well below its market price "provided it went to a body prepared to conserve it".

Then it was balanced against the other contenders. "Various other sites were considered (Powerstock Castle, Eggardon Hill, etc.). A vote was then taken on the island site, to agree (or disagree) in principle to go ahead subject to satisfactory solutions being found to a) management problems, b) fund raising problems. The result of the vote was 3 in favour 1 against," recorded Richard Sandbrook who sat in as our independent secretary. "R.Legg was instructed to continue negotiations on the island." Sandbrook would write to the RSPB about a gull-cull.

Brian Jackman was successful, however, in securing the last decision of the meeting: "It was resolved to keep the Eggardon option open."

First choice: Eggardon Hill (right, with Iron Age ramparts), overlooking the Marshwood Vale in west Dorset, was Ken Allsop's favourite hilltop for birdwatching and the obvious objective for his nature reserve memorial. Seen from the south-east. Photographed by Colin Graham in 1973.

Second choice: Steep Holm, an island in the middle of the Bristol Channel, on which the Kenneth Allsop Memorial Fund set its sights when negotiations failed to buy Eggardon. Seen from the south-west, off Rudder Rock. Photographed by Colin Graham in 1982.

21

The Magus: John Fowles was our wise man, to borrow one of his book titles. His efforts, in terms of persuasion and in providing the finance for his vision, enabled the Kenneth Allsop Memorial Trust to buy Steep Holm. Seen at Belmont House, Lyme Regis, Dorset. Photographed by Colin Graham in 1972.

The next appeal leaflet echoed the indecision: "Ken was above all a fighter for the world about us and his greatest wish would be for that fight to continue. It is intended therefore, that the money to be raised by the appeal should be spent in two ways. First, a piece of land will be acquired in the countryside Ken loved, to be conserved for the benefit of all as a living memorial to him. Currently two possible sites are under consideration, a chalkland hill in Dorset and an island in the Bristol Channel. Both offer great potential as nature reserves. Second, the balance of the Fund will be devoted, under the administration of the charity" – which was Earth Resources Research Limited – "to the research work so urgently needed in the field of environment and resource conservation."

There would be more resistance to the idea of an island. Brian Jackman, Andrew Lloyd Webber, John Percival and I met again in London on 27 November 1973. Richard Sandbrook sat in as our banker and took the minutes:

"R.Legg showed the Committee photographs of the island, Steepholm, and distributed copies of an appraisal of it by John Fowles.

"A. Lloyd Webber reported that the Duchy of Cornwall had been offered the site, but had turned it down because of management problems.

"Management problems were then discussed and it was resolved that a separate group involving R. Legg and J. Percival should meet and report back to the committee.

"R. Sandbrook was instructed to contact a Miss Monica Dixon to act as a paid fund-raiser.

"Brian Jackman reported on two other sites, one in Wiltshire and one in Devon. These were discussed and no further action was decided upon. The meeting closed."

The first, and only, gathering of the "Steep Holm Management Committee" took place at Prospect House, Bruton, on 17 December 1973. John Percival hosted the meeting which was attended by John and Elizabeth Fowles, Amanda Allsop and myself. We set out the basic aims: "To preserve and improve Steep Holm, an exceptional wild life station in the Bristol Channel, as a living memorial to Kenneth Allsop; to establish a bird observatory, enhance and document the island's historical relics; and to encourage summer visitors to enjoy its isolation."

We intended to employ a warden, who would turn out to be Peter Rees, "at £1,000 per annum (lodging free)" – in fact it would be £1,500, and still no rent! Safety concerned us at the beach, particularly the awesome and crumpled metal ladder.

Instead we decided on a "new access road to be made from the beach through the old Inn". Warning notices were agreed for the tops of the steps down to the searchlight posts, and elsewhere something more general: "Dangerous cliffs. Visitors must keep to footpaths."

Public liability insurance was another priority for 1974. A retainer agreement was to be drawn up with the Weston boatmen (Weston being mis-spelt "Western"; none of us was local). The remainder of the decisions would all be attempted or come to pass in greater or lesser measure apart that is from the "working donkey" which was never mentioned again. The meeting even gave me permission to introduce hedgehogs to the island. I did later wonder where I was meant to be "drilling kestrel holes":

"Clearing scrap metal and the mess that comes into vision on landing.

"Path – grubbing rootstocks and ensuring maintenance.

"Barracks – waterproofing the building by repairing the roof and windows.

"Conservation – establishing an observatory in the Barracks to record bird migration movements, and in due course to ring birds.

"Making concrete rainwater pans to provide drinking water for wildlife.

"Publishing – a booklet on all aspects of the island's interests and history, for sale to visitors and supporters of the fund.

"Buying a working donkey for carrying supplies up the cliff path.

"Installing a butane gas cooker in the Barracks, and obtaining quotations for radio equipment.

"Approaching the Royal Artillery Engineers with a view to restoring the guns on their carriages.

"Study – compiling lists of all species of life on the island; seeing what grows on Brean Down and making pilot tests with worthwhile plants.

"Scything the Alexanders and Hemlock in an experimental area to see if prevention of seeding is a realistic consideration.

"Looking into the possibilities of introducing millet, hawthorn, sea buckthorn and other useful food plants; wild daffodils; shrubs; a test number of hedgehogs; in general approaching the Nature Conservancy at Monks' Wood for advice on introduction of species.

"Turning Steep Holm into an open air laboratory for discovering and assessing the ecological impact of various plants and animals and their conditions and needs, and eventually refurbishing the island.

"Making batboxes, drilling kestrel holes, and doing all we can to encourage wildlife."

That was, I think, the only time we formally called ourselves a Steep Holm committee, though John Fowles had suggested establishing "a sort of Friends of Steepholm". There was a certain sensitivity to anything that might displace the Allsop name. John Fowles's draft appeal leaflet was headed "the Steepholm Project".

"I prefer the onwardness of 'project'," he explained, but from the start it made clear that we were raising money for an Allsop memorial rather than an island: "Kenneth Allsop fought passionately to his very last days for our wild life."

John Fowles was careful to ensure that there was an opt-out in the event of a second Eggardon-style failure: "I've discussed this with John Percival, and we both feel – in case the money can't be raised and has to be diverted elsewhere – that it must be made clear Steepholm is an ambition, not a certainty."

It was to relaunch the Allsop Fund, but with Steep Holm as the objective, that we would next meet.

Meanwhile, Richard Sandbrook cautioned realism. "Should we involve ourselves in the purchase of a not-very-threatened island in a remote place just when many other sites are under severe threat?" he asked. "It is the question that worries me now, particularly after discussions over the last two weeks with staff here."

Then he warned that an island was for ever: "It is difficult to project how long Friends of the Earth (and hence Earth Resources Research) will exist (hopefully forever!) but the possibility of it not continuing beyond the Fund's ownership of the island should not be forgotten. Therefore in the long term the management committee will have to take over the total responsibility of the fund." Sandbrook saw two reasons for purchasing Steep Holm. It could be a "place of peace" where people could "recharge their batteries or carry out some work". It would be "a remote reserve for endangered species".

That said, he felt all else was against it. Steep Holm was unthreatened: "This is because it is remote and in an unfavourable location so far as holiday development is concerned." This access problem would make the island elitist, though he was kind enough to phrase it more mildly, as "a memorial for a minority of people to enjoy". It was also expensive in comparison to the "much simpler possibilities offering nature reserve and common enjoyment potentiality". Finally, the dismissive remark that hurt, it was "outside the English countryside that Ken loved and worked within" and "not the priority that Ken would have wished us to pursue".

Sandbrook's realism extended the other way as well. He knew that despite all these reservations there was only one possible conclusion: "If the committee can overtly raise the required capital to purchase the site, then buy it they must."

As for Friends of the Earth: "We are collectively about campaigning, not about land buying. We think it fair therefore that we should resign from the committee altogether except for two reservations."

Firstly, we were to be let off the hook of "past commitments" which would have us owing £17,300 to Earth Resources Research, and that the new committee could "revise their plans for us accordingly". Secondly, "as our name and goodwill are involved, we suggest that Charles Levison, our chairman, sits on the committee from now on. All administrative jobs must be handed over to other committee members if the above is agreed upon."

Charles Levison joined Betty and Amanda Allsop, John Percival, Peter Rees and myself for a meeting with John Fowles at Lyme Regis on 2 February 1974. The "Kenneth Allsop Memorial Fund" had first approached the BBC for an address but had been turned down. Charles Levison said he would check with Richard Sandbrook at Friends of the Earth to see if theirs could be used instead.

Then, after suggesting this cementing of the fund's links with Friends of the Earth, he proceeded to suggest that our closer connection with Earth Resources Research Limited – the use of its bank account – should be unravelled. Amanda Allsop's minutes of the meeting record that he was urging us to become a separate charity:

"Charles Levison asked who would own the island, and whether we were a registered charity. To the first question, Rodney Legg suggested that we appoint ourselves as trustees, with a clause that, should the committee ever fall to pieces, the island is put into the hands of the Society for the Promotion of Nature Reserves.

"Charles Levison felt that we should register ourselves as a charity and call ourselves the Kenneth Allsop Memorial Trust. We would be a limited company, by guarantee, which would insure us. The solicitors negotiating for the island will be able to handle the legalities of this action. There was general approval, though this will mean separating our account from that of Earth Resources Research. Charles Levison will look into the ERR situation, and talk to Richard Sandbrook."

Charles Levison asked all the right questions. His last was to put us on the spot, as Mandy Allsop records: "Charles Levison asked us if we were absolutely certain that the island was the right memorial. Betty Allsop gave the answer for all of us by saying that, had Eggardon been available, for emotional reasons she would have wanted that; but that Ken was a fighter, and that he would take up a challenge and work with all his energy to achieve his end; that birds were his life, his complete love – above, even, human beings – though he was never sentimental about them; and for those reasons, Steep Holm epitomised all that he lived for and believed in and would be the ideal memorial to him."

Between us, as we sprawled in the split-level main downstairs room of Belmont House and waited for the signal to rise for drinks, the distraction was a Wild Peony. It was on a table, smooth to touch but colder even than the big room, and defiantly in flower. This was a porcelain sculpture by Patrick O'Hara who was lending it for use at fund-raising events. I have often wondered what then became of it; everyone was admiring it, and it would have made the perfect centrepiece for the Steep Holm display at Woodspring Museum.

To have acquired it then would have been to tempt fate – we were all aware that there was every possibility that a ceramic peony could well be the closest we would come to owning a piece of Steep Holm.

That month I not only made it clear to the Wharton Estate that the acquisition of the island was now our single objective, but that the Steep Holm Trust lease must not be renewed. My deciding card with the land-agent was a statement about the collapsed roofs at the Barracks which had made the eastern part uninhabitable and was starting to bring down great chunks of the heavy lime ceiling in the main hall. "We would have done something about the repairs," I was told, "if we knew that we would be getting a new lease."

The coup-de-grâce for Edmund Mason, the chairman of the Steep Holm Trust, as far as Baroness Wharton was concerned, was his disturbance of the Priory. He then compounded his dilemma by unwisely adding that the work, news of which had deeply upset the Baroness, "would be continued if the Trust could secure the island on the expiry of the existing lease". The dead, she insisted, had a right to their peace.

27

The Kenneth Allsop Memorial Fund met at Lyme Regis on 23 February 1974 to organise the next stage of the process. "Betty Allsop agreed to take on the task of co-ordinating the campaign, thus eliminating any complications which might arise if committee members acted individually," the minutes record. There was a growing list of eminent patrons whose names were to be printed down the side of the Trust's next edition of notepaper.

John Fowles also minuted my actions, which would bring about the extinction of the Steep Holm Trust: "As the lease of the Steep Holm Trust is near to termination the Wharton estate are considering a renewal of their lease. Rodney Legg has informed our solicitors that we intend to manage the island ourselves, as soon as the contracts have been exchanged. Therefore the solicitors acting for Baroness Wharton should not renew the lease to the Steep Holm Trust."

My faux pas that nearly lost us the island was on the handling of the proposed gull-cull. I realised the damage that it could do to our image, but the mess that colossal numbers of gulls had made of the island seemed to make it imperative. I was stupid enough to put in a letter that would be passed on to Nigel Murray, at Palmer Snell in Yeovil, that they should be shot but that if any reporter phoned up we would claim that "vandals with guns had landed on the island". He was horrified and fortunately prevented any further circulation of the comment. "Baroness Wharton will go through the roof if she ever sees that," he said.

It was hardly a tactful opening gambit anyway, to an elderly lady who had devoted her life to providing free veterinary services for the pathetic creatures the Portuguese half-kept as pets, and looking back it seems madness that we raised it at all. In another memo I had expressed it rather better: "A more positive harm is that these gulls so obviously make the island unattractive to other rock-nesting birds and they are probably an equal nuisance for the rest of the year on the Welsh and Somerset coasts."

Roger House re-phrased the matter for the Baroness but even this version leaves me – a much later convert to full vegetarianism and the non-killing of wildlife – embarrassed and shaking: "The Trust also understand that the number of gulls on the island has grown to a greater number than is in the interests of the future conservancy of gulls on this island because they are of such a number that they will kill themselves off" – in which case why bother? – "and therefore a cull has to be carried out. The Trust will organise this cull in the best way possible having taken advice on the proper methods."

There was a gull-shoot but only for science, the bags of corpses being taken back to Cardiff University for post mortem, and there was indeed a problem with unauthorised shooters. Fresh shotgun cartridge cases were conspicuous across the island. One of the first Girl Guide work parties, from Weston, came under fire from the sea when they were in the trees above the Monks' Well. Shelduck were flying out. The girls' leader was not amused when I postulated the possible newspaper headline: "Brown Owl shot by wildfowlers."

Betty Allsop was the saviour as our fund-raiser. She had only stepped in after others had declined or, as John Fowles wrote in a letter to me about one candidate, "The trouble with Nigel" was that he had adopted the questionable ethics of the mid-1980s a whole decade early. Betty was both an Allsop and she was Betty. She talked the Printmakers Council into donating a whole exhibition of modern art. She charmed the odd £1,000 out of Butlin's holiday camp at Minehead – who never did send us the promised quid pro quo of campers – and a similar cheque from the charity committee of the major banks. Betty also teased one or two directors of the multi-national mineral corporations whom Ken had bashed in Snowdonia. One had saved its reputation in the courts, from as the gentleman put it, "one of the vilest libels ever made against a corporate body". For that reason, he said, there could be no company donation, but he showed forgiveness by enclosing his personal tenner.

Ironically, the worst act of sabotage to be inflicted upon the fund raising efforts was from the successor to the early evening television news programme on which Ken had worked. It was the kind of fait accompli that I might have pulled, except that I didn't and it went far enough to be a disaster. The "Nationwide" team had filmed Steep Holm from a helicopter and a picturesque "newsreel" (the word was still in use, at least by our solicitor) went out at prime-time. The calamity was that the report said the island had now been purchased as Kenneth Allsop's memorial; "has been bought" the voice-over stated.

The whole story was a monumental error and what should have been our greatest publicity coup was entirely counter-productive. There was no longer any reason for people to contribute to an appeal that had reached its target. It blighted what should have been the fund-raising climax, but the "Nationwide" controllers refused to put out a correction over the air, and only conceded an insignificant paragraph in the Radio Times.

Neither, despite the strength of the connection in the public mind between Kenneth Allsop and the BBC, did we ever manage to make the "Week's Good Cause" on Radio-4. The guardian of the Corporation's conscience was adamant that a plan to buy and conserve an island was not the kind of thing that was to be encouraged. "Good gracious," she said, "if we let you broadcast we'd have to say yes to people wanting money for every old church in the land!"

Theodore Goddard, solicitors at St Martin's-le-Grand in London, were handling Baroness Wharton's British affairs. They said she realised appealing for money was a slow process and generously asked us to manage Steep Holm as if the island were already bought. She had, they emphasised, one particular concern, which was to avoid any further disturbance of the remains of the dead. Her faith in the old Steep Holm Trust had ended when she heard about the removal of human bones from the island. It led to me wording an additional clause for the Steep Holm conveyance, requiring the Trust "to request the Department of the Environment to schedule the Priory site for statutory protection under the Ancient Monuments Acts and whether or not the site is granted such legal protection the purchasers as trustees to undertake to preserve the site as if it were their duty in law".

That request was made immediately and Beric Morley, an Inspector of Ancient Monuments, was brought to the island later in 1974 and agreed to make the listing. "I am going to do as you suggest and schedule the Priory," he said. "I will include the ruined cottage and the ground to the west of it as there is a good chance that the mediaeval buildings covered a larger area."

Baroness Wharton also asked for a "piece of rock" from the island as a memento. Thirdly, there was the matter of money – £25,000 was the price, with time to pay.

Betty Allsop had moved from West Milton into Powerstock village, a mile up the valley, and we met there on 6 April 1974. John Fowles minuted the situation: "Rodney Legg reported that (1) the solicitors had in hand the articles of association to do with the Trust (2) they advised that we should not press for exchange of contracts. It was resolved that we should proceed on the assumption that we were granted 'occupation' of the island."

It was on 2 May 1974 that our solicitor, Roger House, received the contract. "Strangely enough, after this long delay, I have now heard from Theodore Goddard and Co in London, and they state that the undertakings " – to preserve the Priory site –

"are agreed and Lady Wharton is very anxious that contracts now be exchanged.

"Thus I enclose the contract for signature either by yourself or whoever may be signing in this matter and you will see that at the top of the first page, there is a blank for the name of the purchaser; perhaps you would put in the proper name that the Trust will then take and then, when you sign, make it clear that your signature is made for and on behalf of the Trust.

"Will you please deal with this straight away and return the contract to me and at the same time, a cheque for five per cent of the purchase price, which of course, will be £1,250. It is understood that completion will be in six months from the exchange of contracts."

Legally and morally it was an intractable problem. Richard Sandbrook's primary obligations were to his own London organisation and staff, who were understandably irritated that so much attention and effort was going into what seemed to them to be, both figuratively and literally, a backwater.

It would also probably have been Ken's wish that the cash raised in his name should have gone instead into Friends of the Earth to encourage high-profile interventionist campaigning on behalf of an increasingly threatened environment. Sandbrook was manoeuvring Friends of the Earth through its own financial crisis and was worried that I was about to embroil him in ours. He realised I was impetuous and liable to sign anything.

The overall trustee behind Friends of the Earth in Britain was General Sir John Hackett. "If you put your name to anything that commits Sir John to a single penny then I'm serving you with a writ," Richard Sandbrook warned me.

Friends of the Earth continued to subsidise us with various office, postage and printing costs, and later, after our final break, would be tolerant of our eventual slow repayments of £1,800 – a pittance in terms of what we had once intended giving them. The appeal leaflet gave no hint that this was not the unanimous choice of the committee. It admitted only to a "problem" arising over that point, after the initial launching of the fund:

"Since then the problem has been in finding a suitable memorial. Everybody felt strongly that it should be a living, growing one, befitting to his passionate concern for the environment and his love of birds and other wildlife. The island of Steep Holm is the ideal monument to Kenneth."

The "Kenneth Allsop Memorial Trust", which was to be the name inserted in the blank space on the conveyance, met on 5

May 1974, at the Belmont House home of John Fowles on the cliffs at Lyme Regis, and the author took its minutes. Present were Betty Allsop, John Percival, Peter Rees, John Fowles and myself. The crucial second item reads: "Rodney Legg brought the contract, and it was signed."

What was not known was that Baroness Wharton had died in Portugal and would be in the obituary column of The Times in the morning. Roger House wrote to me on 7 May saying the solicitors at the London end "will be seeking fresh instructions from Farrar and Co, who are Baroness Wharton's immediate solicitors, and reporting to me again. Until that time, they suggest that I sit on the contract that you have just returned and, of course, your cheque will be paid in here and put on deposit so that interest can accrue. I will be in touch with you again as soon as I can."

The Wharton Barony, which had been created in 1544-45, was in abeyance. Its co-heiresses were the daughters of the last Baroness Wharton, the eldest being Ziki who had married Henry MacLeod Robertson in 1958 and had three sons and a daughter, and the second being Caroline, who had married Commander Jonathan Appleyard-List of the Royal Navy in 1970.

Betty Allsop relaunched the appeal fund in July 1974. Richard Sandbrook had written from Friends of the Earth to tell her that the current balance stood at £4,560 and six thousand leaflets were going out with pre-paid envelopes. "It seems of great importance to me that we try to stimulate some income now before we enter into a contract for the island," Sandbrook wrote. "We have been very disappointed with the response of late to your efforts, but we are finding the same problem." Britain was sliding into recession in the summer of 1974 but it was not only with the state of the country that we were encountering difficulties.

Though it seemed that August had opened well. Mrs Robertson had travelled down from London to view her Bridgwater inheritance, with Nigel Murray, and on Saturday 3 August 1974 she brought the family to the island. What they saw was a mess, the dereliction of the west wing of the Barracks and the complete ruination of its eastern section, and we picked our way along a multiplicity of sub-paths that detoured around the Nissen hut debris at Split Rock and along the entire north-eastern perimeter of the island. Peter Rees and his first work parties had made a start at clearance but from the first we realised that volunteers were only as good as their supervision. Several feet of the south-western corner of the Inn were kicked into the sea by a scout leader who had the novel demolition technique of sitting astride the wall as he removed the stones from between his legs. A potentially usable wartime generator house, the one west of the winch on the southern perimeter path, was wrecked in the name of tidiness.

Mrs Robertson saw that there was endless scope for improvement and left with the vision of an offshore tip – enhanced by the sight and smell of dead gulls and the filth they had carried to the island – rather than the mini-paradise that would captivate the hearts and minds of visitors in the 1980s. Her husband, the composer Harry Robertson, was also keenly in support of the Allsop Fund's efforts. The rest of her "tribe" seemed excited but were too young and city-minded to want to play with a remote island. We were still in the running.

"Will you rename it 'Allsop Island'?" Mrs Roberston asked. I hesitated and said no, adding that Steep Holm had been its identity for centuries. That was, in retrospect, a mistake. Though it would always have caused a tussle for ascendancy between the two names this would have acted as a reminder of the person who had indirectly made our work possible, and whose ideas we were committed to promoting. It would also have offset the inevitable association of us latter-day participants with the island. Mr and Mrs Rendell became synonymous with the Priory in the same way that I would monopolise the television appearances. The losers in this are the Allsop family, who have seen the memorial being overlaid by new associations. In the August of 1974 that was the least of our problems.

Later that month we tasted more of the troubles of running this category of possession. The problems were at every level. Equipment we had been promised by the old Steep Holm Trust had been removed, down to the most useless pieces of old metal, and there had also been a reluctance "to part with the Steep Holm keys, which has meant that several hours of Peter's limited time have been wasted in attacking doors with screwdrivers". The "removal antics" had also left the island without provisions, Peter Rees told me before he zoomed off again to be stranded there by a gale in the second week of August.

That, for us at least, removed the Steep Holm Trust as rival candidates for another lease. Stephen Cook, for solicitors Withers, made it clear on 19 August 1974 that the sympathy of the owners was now firmly with us: "I was very disappointed to hear about the 'raid' on the island. Do let me know if you think there is any way in which I can help."

Yet one sensed that this clever young man, in the heart of London's law-land, was going to make sure that in another couple of decades we were not going to be making our own shambolic exit to the mainland. We were being shifted from potential buyers into de facto lessees, with a document that would have ensured that on our departure there would be the threat of a frightening claim for dilapidations. Neglect had put us as front-runners for the occupancy, mainly because the Barracks gutters were growing the only lush grass on the island, and thanks to the previous tenants' accumulation of tin-cans and old paint tins beside, above and even inside its only reservoir tank. Some of them had even been using the well-head as their lavatory! Repetition was a valid worry for the owners.

The position in October 1974 was that the Kenneth Allsop Memorial Fund committee was reluctantly considering the possibility that it might be allowed only to rent Steep Holm. Stephen Cook started with the suggestion of a twenty-one year lease and a £5,000 premium. He later told Roger House, acting for the Allsop Fund, that this was only an opening gambit. He was prepared to extend the term to forty years but resisted anything longer. Whilst happy, he said, with the present enthusiasm and intentions of the organisation, he wanted some protection for the owners so that they could enforce the covenants if the situation had changed for the worse in ten or twenty years

They left us to discuss the matter. I wrote to Betty Allsop, John Fowles and John Percival on 16 October 1974 and shared the bad news:

"My main disappointment is because we had been led to expect something a lot kinder. Had we not appeared on the scene, according to Mrs Robertson's agent, the existing Steep Holm Trust would have been allowed to continue at something like its previous 50p a week.

"Can we afford £800 yearly for 40 years? Or should we offer them £10 a week and promise that we will maintain and repair the Barracks which, after all, is the island's main asset if it ever came to an auction. Obviously we had better meet, but in the meantime I'll do nothing to commit us to anything."

As the work out at sea moved into three dimensions the situation in London impressed no one; the fund did not have a separate existence. It was still a book-keeping entry in Earth Resources Research Limited which operated as the charity-wing of the Friends of the Earth. Our banker and provider of offices was Richard Sandbrook who maintained a guarded neutrality over the eventual form the memorial would take.

Following her visit to the island, Mrs Robertson again met John Percival and myself, but this time in the London offices of her solicitors, off the Strand. Stephen Cook, of Withers, set out the legal alternatives. He suggested that if we could not raise sufficient money for an outright purchase – not even approaching the £25,000 we had agreed to pay Baroness Wharton – then we could instead have the option of a long lease. That, at ninety-nine years, struck John and me as a rather temporary memorial.

On Stephen's memorandum of the meeting it had been hedged with qualifications. There was a clause requiring a "realistic rent, perhaps coupled with a premium, provided your clients can satisfy Mrs Robertson that they are in a strong enough financial position at that time to do this" – the key word was "provided", and to make sure it was seen as such Stephen had it put into capital letters and underlined. Initially, however, they were prepared to have us as licensees, continuing to occupy and improve the island on the existing rent-free basis for "perhaps four years".

There was also the problem that Stephen Cook did not like the linkage of the Allsop memorial appeal with the ecological pressure group Friends of the Earth:

"Added to this, there are obviously difficulties arising from the Trust's association with the Friends of the Earth. I understand that there are some reciprocal moral obligations between these two organisations as to the allocation of funds or part of the funds which have been collected, and unless this situation is clarified very quickly, I foresee the Kenneth Allsop Memorial Trustees running into difficulties with the Revenue and the Charity Commissioners, and in any event, I would have thought that your clients would wish to know exactly where they stand on this."

The last hiccup in the transfer of means from the accounts of Earth Resources Research to the newly independent Allsop Fund, during the winter of 1974, was my "foolhardy" intervention with the Charity Commission. I argued that a slice of the moneys which, I claimed, had been directly raised from the public on the basis that it would be used for some "suitable memorial" in the form of land, had been applied to more general purposes. Richard Sandbrook conceded the point, in a letter to my solicitors on 30 April 1975: "Whilst I fully appreciate your concern to impress the Charity Commissioners with the fact that we should pay back the £2,000 transferred from one account to another, I am a little unhappy with the way it was done." He had expressed his opinion much more strongly by telephone but the letter, fortunately, ended in a conciliatory tone: "I am so glad that the whole island project now seems possible."

Whilst we were always able to impress the Environment Department, there was little love left to lose between the Kenneth Allsop Memorial Trust and the Nature Conservancy Council. Before they had fully realised the Allsop connection they were abundant with helpful information, from Monks' Wood and Taunton, about the reasons why the island had been designated a Site of Special Scientific Interest (SSSI) under the National Parks and Access to the Countryside Act of 1949. Then, on 2 April 1975, the World Wildlife Fund shelved "Project 22/75 – Steep Holm Island" because we were being disowned in high places. "The application was deferred for further enquiries from the Nature Conservancy Council as to the validity of the island being classified as an SSSI," Miss V.C. Craig told me. "Perhaps you would like to look into this."

Nothing about our representations and plans, either from the approaches in London or the actual work on the island, had filtered through to the people in the Conservancy who should have been made aware of this. "Recent discussions with the local representative of the Nature Conservancy Council suggest that you have had little if any contact with them," Avon Planning Department told me.

Then a harassed London official admitted that we had been blocked by bureaucratic resistance induced by the Allsop name. "He caused us more trouble than any other person," the unattributable male source confessed. "He would pull up directly outside in his E-type and storm in and demand to see the Director-General. There would be phone calls and angry confrontations, accusing people of not caring and being ignorant. People here remember that sort of thing, particularly when it's led to a reprimand from above for something he had gone on about."

Publicly the opposition melted. An old friend from my London days a decade before, Miss Nettie Bonnar, was still in a key position at the Conservancy's national headquarters in Belgrave Square. She wrote me the Conservancy's official words of welcome, on 16 May 1975: "We are of the opinion that, under suitable management it is quite likely that the scientific interest and educational potential of the site could be further developed: if the Trust does acquire the island, therefore, the Nature Conservancy Council would welcome the opportunity to discuss with them how this might best be achieved."

Privately, resistance remained. The World Wildlife Fund was not sufficiently convinced, and did not part with any money, and the Nature Conservancy remained impervious to requests for positive support. Ten years later the problem remained and a grant-aid application, suggested by one of their officials, received only a single postcard acknowledgement. By 1975 we had higher hopes of making contact, via a Grand Cayman address, with "Union Jack" Hayward who had bought Lundy Island for the nation and brought the *Great Britain* home from the Falkland Islands, up-Channel past Steep Holm.

On the island, the Post Office had brought warden Peter Rees a radio telephone to his quarters at the west end of the Barracks, in August 1974. He was to put it to effective use at the end of the month: "Telephone contact was maintained throughout the night of 1st September with the coastguards at Barry on the Welsh coast. Storm force winds lashed the West Country and there was a succession of alarms for lost boats. In the early hours, a 15-foot cabin cruiser was washed ashore on the shingle bank below the island's eastern cliffs. We rushed into the water with 300 feet of rope and helped ashore two men and three boys. It was only with extreme difficulty that we eventually managed to drag their boat ashore. They insisted on leaving us later that night, and returning to the gale, and the last we heard of them was their second rescue, at dawn, by a party of policemen who had to wade across the mud of Newport estuary."

John Fowles concentrated our minds on 31 January 1975 with a "Strategy" for the future. The immediate objectives were to "gain legal possession" of the island – we were already wardening it by licence – and "to establish our own charity status". Betty Allsop was needing to step down as the fund raiser but we would never replace her with anyone in Weston, or anywhere, who met the requirements – "efficient and literate and retired". There were also problems of distance, plus age and personality differences, with Peter Rees feeling out-of-touch with an absentee and impoverished committee. He also had, in John Fowles's words, a "distaste for letter-answering" which was already leading me to be plagued with requests to arrange Steep Holm visits, which would punctuate my life for thirteen years – eventually leading me to refuse to answer the telephone except for three hours on Friday evenings – until Joan Rendell rashly offered her number instead.

The commitment, as John Fowles saw it, was for "clearance,

repair and habitat-improvement" on the island to be complemented by an accumulation of knowledge. Peter was to be encouraged "to start a proper species-list index" and John gave him a couple of stout box-files. "And can Rodney make copies of the past scientific papers to start an island library?" That afterthought was the precursor of these books. Knowledge, as you will by now have realised, is the only commodity that is not subject to diminishing returns.

Whilst we gathered facts, others responded with flak. Reports filtering back to Bristol about the island led to reactions discoloured by acrimony and disinformation. For the lavatorial aside we had naturalists complaining that "tomatoes are growing in many places on the island because of the deposition of seeds from human excreta, circumstances arising from the failure to provide toilets". That was ironic, given that in 1974 and in every year since I have on at least one occasion had my hands down a blocked manhole, and that from the start the Allsop Trust set about reintroducing the water-closet to Steep Holm. By 1986 there would be six such installations in working order, thanks to Doug Tripp, Ken Cass and Mike Prangle.

More hurtful were the barbs that led to ill-informed official condemnation, such as the censorious intervention of Cherry Copperwheat on 17 April 1975, writing from the upstart "County of Avon". She was doubting our abilities at all levels: "As a Planning Department we are becoming increasingly more involved in matters of nature conservation and countryside management, together with aspects of rural recreation. Indeed we are in the process of setting up a small group of specialists within the department to advise on such matters. As a member of this group I am concerned at the apparent lack of expertise within the Kenneth Allsop Memorial Trust, or available to it, to advise on the management of Steep Holm, which is after all a valuable national site for nature conservation."

The letter was written "For the County Planning Officer" and it would be my disappointment in the years that followed that we never enticed H.E. Stutchbury to the extremity of his domain. My subsequent visits to Bristol have convinced me that the absence of its planners has been to the eternal benefit of the aesthetics on Steep Holm. Sadly, almost, such stimulating letters are now a thing of the past. People no longer dare to write them to me. Once bitten, no one writes to me again.

The natural history fraternity appeared to be at one against us, but the morale booster for the difficult autumn of 1974 was that nature thought otherwise. Given Kenneth Allsop's admiration for the agile flight and the sound barrier-breaking woosh of the Peregrine stoop, it was the most thrilling discovery, by Peter Rees on 27 September, that these magnificent predators had returned to the island. These were the first confirmed sightings since 1956 and they coincided with a pair of Ravens also tentatively prospecting the island for an eventual breeding return. The omens were promising.

One of the most exciting moments of my life was the confirmation from our Bournemouth solicitor, Roger House, that Mrs Robertson's solicitors had been "absolutely splendid and rather surprising" in accepting our offer for the island. It was surprising because it was not much of an offer. Basically, it set out the reality, which was that the fund raising carried out by Betty Allsop and the Friends of the Earth secretarial team had raised £15,000. John Fowles had brought it to that level with a magnificent gift of £1,500.

The problem, however, was paying for 1974. That would be the only time the island project would employ a full-time warden, Peter Rees from Puncknowle in Dorset, and there were the constant stream of work parties who had to be ferried to the island. In round figures, that was going to account for £3,500, and then we had to pay Friends of the Earth £1,500 for time, offices, printing and postage. It left only a meagre offering for one of nature's rarest pieces of real estate – an offshore English island.

"£10,000 won't buy a semi-detached house in Ealing," John Percival remarked.

I had put the problem to Mrs Robertson but without mentioning the slimness of the remaining figure. "Don't worry," she said, "There isn't a problem. You can pay us what you have left in the fund."

That was so little, it verged almost upon an insult, but Stephen Cook wrote from Withers, at Essex Street in the Strand, to finalise the matter of "Steep Holme Island" in the terms Mrs Robertson had so generously conceded. He told Roger House on 8 April 1975:

"I have now obtained instructions from Mrs Robertson and Messrs Hoare Trustees in respect of the offer made subject to contract by your client of £10,000 for the freehold of this Island.

"Subject to my comment about costs below, Mrs Robertson and Hoare Trustees are willing to accept your client's offer for the Island.

"I know that both you and your client will appreciate the degree of my involvement on behalf of Mrs Robertson in the negotiations over the Island in the hope that an acceptable solution to the problems of the Island generally and the problems of your clients in particular could be found. As a result of this, in addition to Palmer Snell and Co's fee as selling agent, and Messrs Theodore Goddard and Co's normal conveyancing costs, Mrs Robertson has incurred my firm's charges which I estimate will amount to approximately £500. In all the circumstances of this unusual situation Mrs Robertson has asked if your clients will consider making a contribution of say £250 to my firm's costs.

"As I have said above, subject to a resolution on this point, Mrs Robertson is prepared to accept your client's offer subject to contract." Woopee! I excitedly telephoned our chairman.

The connection with John Fowles was changing my life. From 1975 Dorset Publishing Company, which I ran as a partnership with the talented photographer Colin Graham, diversified into local antiquarian books, manuscripts and prints under the trade-name "Dorsetiana". John Fowles was a regular buyer, particularly after he became curator of the fossil-packed town museum in Lyme Regis, though there was some sales resistance on 10 November 1977: "Get thee behind me, thou Satan of Sherborne – decided last week to stop buying so many books, just never get round to reading most of them. Cheque enclosed! J. Have always wanted it in fact." More constructively, my research into the unpublished magnum opus of early British archaeology, John Aubrey's *Monumenta Britannica* from the seventeenth century, would lead to John Fowles and I publishing the first edition of that work in 1981-82. John was completing *The Enigma of Stonehenge*, in the course of which he became fascinated with another piece of writing from the 1660s, *A Fool's Bolt Soon Shott at Stonage*.

There was, coincidentally, a mention of it in Aubrey's "hopelessly ill-organised" notes which we had at last released into general circulation after three centuries of incarceration in the Bodleian Library. This led us to Nettlecombe Court, in the foothills of Exmoor, where we were able to place the credit for the *Fool's Bolt* on Robert Gay. The detective work that cracked the puzzle was published in 1986 as the introduction to my book on the *Stonehenge Antiquaries*.

At Nettlecombe there was a further coincidence. It was now owned by the Field Studies Council and Dr John Crothers ran the Leonard Wills Field Study Centre. In the grounds he was able to show John Fowles a cage of Steep Holm banded snails which were under observation to confirm that their unexpectedly large size and bright colours were due to genetic rather than environmental differences. John Fowles treated John Aubrey's maze of puzzles "as a change from the crossword" and for me it was a substitute for the university education I had missed.

Monumenta Britannica became for both of us a collection of "beautiful Aubreyisms" and John Fowles enthused over the hoard of otherwise lost facts and John Aubrey's long-underrated brilliance of natural style. "He once wrote this," John Fowles pointed out: " 'I did see Mr Christopher Love beheaded on Tower Hill in a delicate clear day.' All his genius lies in this unexpected 'delicate'. I have long held it the most pleasing short sentence in the language."

The other achievement in print of the collaborations of the Fowles years was the creation of the first book to be written about Steep Holm. I was the hack and he the wordsmith and editor for *Steep Holm – a case history in evolution* which was published in 1978 and would earn the Trust £2,500 by the time it went out-of-print.

One of its complimentary mentions in a scientific environment was the review by R.J.Berry in the journal Biologist for February 1980: "Ten of the seventeen chapters have been written by Rodney Legg, secretary of the Allsop Trust, who is clearly an enthusiast for the island after the mould of Joe Eggeling, Kenneth Williamson, or Frank Fraser Darling for their particular isolates; other chapters are contributed by a variety of people, including the novelist John Fowles, himself a naturalist and friend of Kenneth Allsop.

"My memory of Steep Holm is of an island overrun by nettles and herring gulls. It is good that it is now in hands eager to exploit it for worthy biological ends – I include aesthetic and conservation aims with 'biological'."

The format of the book and its design was largely due to Colin Graham's influence and efforts. The catalyst was the discovery of a whole new field of research at the same time as I had expanded the knowledge of the Second World War fortification of the island with an account of the memories of soldiers involved. Until that time no one even seemed to know that it had taken place in July 1941. As for the scientific matter, that concerned snails as the proof of Darwinism, and was the subject of a Science Research Council grant, leading to some tittering in Parliament and a cartoon I have unfortunately lost. "After all," it was captioned "it may have applications for British Leyland."

Colin Graham saw Cuillin Bantock's snail research as the

symbol of new positivism and use of the island. It was high-grade and exciting, continuing the work of our greatest naturalist, and it marked the departure from the vagueness of the past. Apart from Ray Poulding's splendid work we had inherited not even the semblance of a species list. Indeed, my island inventory from the old Steep Holm Trust showed an inability even to count the gun barrels: "At least 6 Victorian cannon at Steep Holm." It was dated May 1969, twenty years after they had taken over the island, when eight of these cannon were then visible.

Colin saw that snails were the perfect answer. They were at once neither cuddly, popular nor folksy. Few people (Cuillin Bantock excepted) would study snails with an outpouring of emotion. It was therefore Colin's decision that the snail report had to be the opening chapter, and sub-title justification, for our book *Steep Holm – a case study in the history of evolution* which was the first full-size book, of 226 pages, to be devoted to the island. We claimed it as a "record of all that is known about Steep Holm", which is an impossible claim, but in the event it proved close enough. The book contains ninety-five per cent of the knowledge at the time. We had missed little and less of significance.

John Fowles, our editor, was also enthusiastic: "I am delighted the snail man has turned up trumps. It would be marvellous if we turn out to have a small modern repeat of Darwin in the Galapagos. His finches and our snails!"

The continuing legacy of my first years of wardening Steep Holm was the introduction of two additional species of mammals, doubling that category of life-forms on the island, with consignments of hedgehogs and Muntjac deer. These were to arouse a storm from Somerset and Bristol naturalists. The principle of adding to the island's somewhat impoverished land-fauna had already been set by John Fowles, though he was thinking of a somewhat smaller species when he wrote to me on 30 April 1975:

"While I'm rambling on, there is a splendid Continental spider introduction that has succeeded – a very striking creature called *Argiope bruennichi* – and we must try to establish it. Bristow reports two Hampshire colonies. I know it only from the Mediterranean, but obviously it will survive here. It has a remarkable web, and is a daylight creature; so just what we need."

I had already introduced a boot-load of hedgehogs to the island and John Fowles was anxious about snail-man Bantock's reaction. Fortunately this was mild: "Hedgehogs most certainly eat snails (they crush and swallow them whole), but I think not very regularly. They hunt by smell. I don't think the introduction will seriously affect the snails unless they become extremely common."

"I find myself more and more intrigued by this island," Dr Cuillin Bantock told us. "So much of the fauna seems to fit in with Darwin's observations on island fauna on his voyage – large size being common where predation is low. You notice that a spider species is large. I noticed that the woodlice are much bigger than on the mainland. I collected a few in 1972 and measured them; they were several millimetres bigger than the upper figure for the maximum length given in the keys. I really do think that the invertebrate fauna should be examined systematically and more extensively."

I told John Fowles in April 1975 that I was going to collect the next batch of endangered hedgehogs that I encountered on main roads in north Dorset; I wanted to pick-up the females before they had nests of young. He wrote back on 15 April 1975: "Hedgehogs will need a good pile of brushwood for hibernating – and water?"

On 27 April 1975, John Fowles warned me about the claims for 1974 that I had re-written in Peter Rees's name in my revised version of his annual report: "I appreciate the need to 'sell' the island, but I object to the too high expectations and claims raised in this report. When so much can be checked on by a sharp-eyed visitor, it's asking for trouble."

In particular the list of work projects implied these had been carried out, when at best they were in progress, but they would all be achieved in the phenomenal burst of continuous energy that was expended on the island through the coming season. On their next trip John and Elizabeth Fowles overcame most of their pessimism: "Enjoyed our trip. I think the old sod will be a credit to us yet."

Things were happening on the island on the biggest scale since the summer of 1941. I had become warden in place of Peter Rees – involuntarily, part-time and boatless. Peter's Jacques Cousteau style Zodiac Mark-2 inflatable languished in my garden, and then with John Fowles at Lyme Regis, as we decided that the only access arrangement with pensionable possibilities was to give the experienced Watts family of boatmen from Weston the ferry monopoly.

Groups working on the restoration project included the International Voluntary Service, Forest School Camps, Sidcot School, several teams of guides and Weston Sea Cadets. A high proportion were girls and most of the volunteers were aged between thirteen and twenty. Perhaps their greatest achievement was the removal of more than 2,500 cubic feet of stone and earth to expose an entirely covered Victorian gun emplacement at Garden Battery. The filling had been dumped there in 1941, and its clearance involved moving the heavy wartime concrete range-finding pillar on which a brass memorial plate to Harry Cox is fixed. This now stands beside the barbette, in a far more attractive setting. The work won an award of merit in the Better Britain Competition.

In the summer of 1975 the gull numbers were well down, but the first of the two drought years exhausted the adult birds trying to ferry in food from the tips, and the chicks along with the human workers digging up so much of the island were pathetically parched. Dead chicks littered the island; there would be few immature gulls flying from the island either that year or the next, and the third year would be too late for any recovery.

The human disturbance was also a powerful disincentive, as seemed to be proved by the fact that the gull population on Flat Holm was rising as ours declined (though it was also relevant that Flat Holm lies much closer to big mainland tips). John Fowles wrote: "Silly of us not to realise that the one successful gull-limiting species of vermin was the human being; all that talk of goats and stoats."

There was national television coverage for our international team of volunteers sweltering in the tropical heatwave to change the appearance of the island. "I thought the TV bit came over very well," John Fowles remarked, "and hardly recognised the dear old place."

In another note, of 10 August 1975, John Fowles had enthused over a little creature that is illustrated in plate 9 of the Collins Field Guide *Insects of Britain*: "I'm really writing because I have hit on an insect we ought to have on the island. It is the Firebug, *Pyrrhocorus apterus*, small, but a pretty carmine and black fellow. It is very rare here – only one permanent colony in Devon, a generally much more southerly distribution, but is dependent on the Tree-mallow for food. It seems just right, being attractive, rare and needing a plant we have in quantity. Do you know any entomologist who might know the Devon site's location? Anyway, let's bear it in mind."

On 20 October 1975, he was checking on the dimensions of a spider he had found on the island: "The female *Atypus* I measured yesterday, the Purse-Web, is 3 mm. (or 25 per cent) over the given size in Lockett and Killidge, by the way; and since I found two other even larger tubes whose occupiers I couldn't extract I suspect the size may run larger still. The tube-ends in the new colony are all buried under rocks; another departure from the norm. A marked difference of special adaptation if not another Steep Holm subspecies yet!"

1975 was the year of the Steep Holm sea-change. I had brought nearly a thousand visitors across to the island. Tony Parsons had ringed more than 500 birds.

The mammoth work programme had excavated tons of earth, rubble and other debris from the barbettes of the Victorian emplacements at Garden Battery, Split Rock, and Summit Battery in particular – including the emptying of the western underground magazine at Summit. There was nothing showing of it at that time, above ground, but I guessed its entrance to the foot, though a whole series of hunches at Garden Battery led only to fruitless digging.

Beric Morley, the inspector of Ancient Monuments – they had just scheduled Split Rock and Rudder Rock – came back and congratulated us on making so much presentable; "It's an impressive transformation. Everything was hidden on our last visit. There's not much more I can ask you to do."

John Fowles inspected the island as we locked up for the year, and contributed the best accolade: "Much enjoyed our visit . . . I think you've contrived miracles this summer."

Before we would see it again, John Fowles and I signed the conveyance to buy, on behalf of the newly incorporated Kenneth Allsop Memorial Trust Limited, "all that piece or parcel of land known as Steep Holm Island situate in the County of Avon being OS Nos 8367 and 0666 on the Ordnance Survey map." It is dated 25 March 1976. It was signed in the south-facing main ground floor room of Belmont House at Lyme Regis. The covenants are strict and the downside of the give-away price:

"a) To restrict the use of the property hereby conveyed to scientific observation and research relating to flora fauna ornithology archaeology geology and botany.
"b) To use its best endeavours to (i) Encourage natural and cultivated growth of the wild peony; (ii) Preserve the foundation of the 12th Century Augustinian Priory; (iii) Keep all items excavated during archaeological research in a suitable place; (iv) Provide a conservation environment for flora and fauna at all times.
"c) Not to remove from the property hereby conveyed the eight [now nine!] muzzle loading Victorian Cannon or the

45

Georgian 32 pounder [actually 24 pounder] Cannon used
as pivots.
"d) Not to carry out any activity commercial or
otherwise that conflicts or is at variance with the
research and scientific interests on the property hereby
conveyed or which is outside the range of activities
implied as relating to the Department of the
Environment's scheduling [in fact the Nature
Conservancy Council's] of the property hereby conveyed
as being of Special Scientific Interest."

A distinguished graphical designer, Michael Harvey of Bridport, carved a plaque in Welsh slate to commemorate Kenneth
Allsop and the buying of the island. The stone he used was
lifted from a Victorian prison floor. Apparently this is now the
best way of acquiring a large slab of high-quality slate. Weighing about 80 pounds, it was mounted by the Trust's engineer,
Michael Yesson, with the help of Tony Parsons, on the vertical
wall of Cliff Cottage, facing eastward and out to sea. It has as its
emblem a Peregrine and records: "This island of Steep Holm
was bought by public subscription in the year 1976 to preserve
the memory of the writer and naturalist KENNETH ALLSOP,
1920-1973."

John Fowles hoped that one day the Trust would plant a bed
of Wild Peony beneath it. It was, and is, the famous plant of the
island, so we were sensitive to the implications for credibility of
the Trust's management of the island if, during our time, it
finally became extinct.

It is offshore where the island is always liable to produce its
biggest surprises. The five foot high erect, pointed back-fin of
an adult male Killer Whale, *Orcinus orca*, emerged from a bank
of mist on the morning of 17 April 1976. It appeared on the
starboard side of a small blue boat packed with day trippers,
which had overshot the island in a fog. The animal, which must
have been 25 feet long, was in the deep-water shipping lane
about a mile north-west of Rudder Rock. On that same trip, the
island's ferry also had close encounters with the *Balmoral*
steamer and a large tanker, being tossed in their wakes. "It was
like a Conrad novel," Colin Graham remembered. My impres-
sionist moment from that day was looking up at that tanker and
being able to see neither its bow nor the stern which were both
in the fog. Between them, seemingly in slow motion, a seaman
was walking the length of the ship. They were gone and Ian
Watts had to contend with their wake.

Medlar: a young tree, bought by Kenneth Allsop for his garden, stands behind his stone in the country churchyard at Powerstock in west Dorset. Photographed by Colin Graham in 1977.

Lest we forget: those of us who enjoy Steep Holm, or merely have public access to it, do so because it was bought 'to preserve the memory' of author and naturalist Kenneth Allsop. The inscription was set in a wall at Cliff Cottage and is seen from the north-east. Photographed by Colin Graham in 1977.

Falcon artwork: the Peregrine logo of the Kenneth Allsop Memorial Trust fortuitously coincided with the bird's return to the island to breed. Drawn by Paul Heath with lettering by Colin Graham, in 1978.

STEEP HOLM

TO PROTECT, PRESERVE AND ENHANCE FOR THE BENEFIT OF THE PUBLIC THE LANDSCAPE, ANTIQUITIES, FLORA, FAUNA, NATURAL BEAUTY AND SCIENTIFIC INTEREST OF THE ISLAND OF STEEP HOLM IN THE COUNTY OF AVON AND TO ADVANCE THE EDUCATION OF THE PUBLIC IN THE NATURAL SCIENCES.

KENNETH ALLSOP TRUST

Kenneth Allsop Memorial Trust Limited was incorporated on 24 September 1975, and is registered in Wales, number 1227940. It was founded in memory of the naturalist and broadcaster Kenneth Allsop, who died in 1973. Registered charity number 270059.

47

Beached: the boating family from Weston-super-Mare making landfall on Steep Holm. John Watts stands in the bows of the *Jane*. Frank Watts is to the left of the plank and Ian Watts, his son, on the other side. *Jane* still sails, off north Devon, and the plank is also a great survivor. Seen from the west. Photographed by Colin Graham in 1976.

Rows over guns and deer

The island had its occasional moments in the news. They were times that John Fowles, already reclusive, wished it did not exist.

"Big guns stand fast" – a headline in The Guardian ran on 8 June 1976. Nikki Knewstub reported that we were proud of our Palmerston Follies and their "last of the muzzle-loaders" that still stood high at the entrance to the Bristol Channel:

"Which is why Mr Rodney Legg, the Trust's secretary, went off with a bang, metaphorically speaking, when he was appraised of the plans by the Glynn Vivian Art Gallery and Museum in Swansea for one of his precious cannon. The museum's curator, Mr John Bunt, wrote to the Trust asking for one.

"Swansea is presenting the Royal Monmouthshire Regiment (Royal Engineers) with the freedom of its broad avenues and the engineers thought it would be a jolly nice idea to present the city with a nice 1868 muzzle-loading cannon. In fact the army had agreed to letting them have a landing craft to transport the gun once it had been hoisted 250 ft down Steep Holm's namesake cliffs. They all agreed that June 26 would be a good day to do it.

"Mr Legg was not amused at the prospect of losing one-eighth of his prize Victoriana. And he said so. Or rather, he wrote: 'This is a reprehensible request. As curator of a respected museum you should be ashamed at conspiring in the proposed rape of the Bristol Channel islands.'

"He threatened to tell the Inspectorate of Ancient Monuments about Mr Bunt's proposed 'raid', adding that plundering intact sites for ancient treasures was not in fashion. Although the request showed that 'the disease is still alive and flourishing in the tiny minds of a Welsh municipality'".

Regarding my admonition of the Swansea authorities, which was a notification that they were to get stuffed, I received a supportive letter from Miss A.L. Tunbridge of the Ancient Monuments Secretariat of the Department of the Environment:

"I have seen copies of your correspondence with Swansea Art Gallery. Thank you for this information. We are of course in sympathy with your view on this. Perhaps you could confirm that none of the cannon have been removed."

Yes, I did take the precaution of going around the island to count the guns on our next visit after 26 June 1976. The press enjoyed the English-Welsh dimension to the broadsides. "If these small-minded Welshmen must have a gun propped outside their city hall they should buy one at auction," the Western Daily Press quoted me as saying. "It's like the British Museum asking if they could take one of the stones from Stonehenge."

Things were going well for the Peregrine. Though we were elated at its return to Steep Holm – it had already been adopted by the Trust as its symbol – John Fowles was pessimistic about the prospect of its breeding on the island again, or the Raven either. He wrote to me on 4 November 1976: "Reducing populations nationally have a choice of optimum sites, and neither bird is fond of humans anywhere near its nest. I think in all honesty you must point out that the chances of either bird keeping a nest on Steep Holm are incompatible with a policy of frequent summer visiting."

He was about to be proved wrong on both counts. In the case of the Raven its breeding cycle starts so early in the year that it has young by the time the first human visitors arrive in the spring. Though he was unaware of the fact, numbers of both birds were increasing from 1975 onwards, and many other of their old stations would also be reoccupied. Tony Parsons doubted if our intrusions, and the consequent key-key-key protests of the birds, would be decisive. "One of the new mainland sites is right above a caravan camp," he said.

John Fowles had written something very nice about me on 2 December 1976: "You are strictly not to cut the little passage in praise of one Rodney Legg, by the way! Being English, we never say these things face to face; but I insist that it is said in print."

Then he had a whole winter of defending me, from the fallout resulting from the leak to the press and television that a herd of Muntjac deer had been released upon the island. I shall outline the events in the order in which the Trust's committee came to hear of them – long after they were fait accompli. "The Muntjac affair" rumbled on and, John Fowles wrote on 18 March 1977, "I think Rodney realises the damage he has done to confidence, not only among ourselves but in terms of any future discovery on the island. In his defence I should like to say that I know better than anyone the enormous amount of work he has put into running the Trust, and I cannot blame him for sometimes feeling that he has to carry its daily burdens and decisions single-handed."

He called for a decision over introductions and set out the arguments on each side:

"Scientifically, most opinion seems against tampering with the present ecology in any way. Because of its isolated position Steep Holm represents a valuable natural laboratory, where species fluctuation and the rest can be observed with a minimum of human interference. The fact that most of the current dominant plants were formerly introduced is irrelevant now. We should therefore run the island according to its scheduling, as a site of special scientific interest, and regard our main 'customers' as serious naturalists and their societies, not those who merely want a pleasant outing. The two aims are not of course necessarily incompatible: I am sure one could interest at least some of the public in a reserve run on strict 'pure-ecology' grounds – and it might well be argued that the sort of visitor who wants a mini-Longleat is in any case best discouraged. To be fair, I should add that the Nature Conservancy did in 1975 sanction the idea of introduction.

"The counter-argument is that we must try to attract a wider range of visitors and that the present (to the layman) rather monotonous ecology needs diversifying. The Trust is a memorial to Kenneth Allsop, and we should not forget that a main preoccupation of his life was to make the general public more interested in nature. Such a purpose is written into the articles of the Trust; and our new *Mini-guide* does of course present the island along these lines.

"We must also understand Rodney's practical view: that the island will never earn its keep unless we maintain a steady flow of summer visitors, and 'attractions' for them. It cannot be run, even with the greatest economy, for nothing; and it is very possible that running it as the old Steep Holm Trust did, strictly for other naturalists, might land us in their final predicament . . . a crippling lack of funds. In a nutshell, we have to decide who the Trust is running the island for, in terms of visitors – whether as a layman's or a naturalist's preserve."

The debate evolved into the creation of a management plan, placing strict curbs on future introductions but otherwise enshrining much of the conservation work that was being carried out anyway, which as far as I know has not been breached – apart from the antics of rogue naturalists who have continued the annual custom of slicing off unripe Wild Peony seed-heads, and on the occasion of a high-level visit had to be reprimanded for climbing down the cliff towards the Peregrine nest. Rules, it has turned out, are for others.

To "enhance" Steep Holm is one of the Trust's foremost objectives, written into its articles of association, and I was delighted when we were offered the chance to enrich the island's rather limited wildlife in 1977. Dr Oliver Dansie, who said he was Kenneth Allsop's physician in Hertfordshire, generously donated the Trust some Muntjac deer, *Muntiacus reevesi*. Betty Allsop later insisted he had never been Ken's doctor; it was an added unforeseen complication, as both were adamant.

The animals were rescued from a wood where they were due to be shot. Dr Dansie was the country's leading expert on this species of deer. The catch-up was approved by the Nature Conservancy and the British Deer Society, but the circumstances allowed no time for consultation within the Trust, and the question of the animals' suitability and fate became entirely my responsibility.

"Operation Muntjac" was carried out over two days with the aid of a hired van and a special January boat trip in 1977 that only just delivered the beasts ahead of a gale. Two things nearly went wrong. The catch-up had netted a serious imbalance of the sexes. At dusk after a very long day I was told that our crates contained three males but only one female.

With all our hopes on her we headed west and lodged the animals for the night in Ian Watts's porch. Next morning we staggered down Anchor Head but the loading was trickier, with me jumping into the sea after the crate containing the female lurched into the water between the slipway and the heaving bow of the boat. At the other end, Colin Graham and Ron Porter, followed by Ian and myself, carried the two double-crates – which had been made to fit a Landrover rather than a boat, and were definitely not designed for lifting up a mountain – on to the top of the island. We released them on the path between Tombstone Battery and the Farmhouse and they walked gently, as exhausted and shaken-up as we were, into the scrub. The female looked back at me. It was all over bar the telephone calls.

Peter Carne, the editor of the journal named Deer, called them "an intriguing addition indeed to the island's fauna".

They are tiny animals, not much larger than a fox, and are a living fossil. Though the present Muntjac wild in England and Wales are the successors of animals brought from China, that escaped from deer parks, there were almost identical animals in Europe 35 million years ago. They are the only surviving representative of an enormous group of extinct mammals, the Palaeomerycidae. Dr Dansie pointed out that the Muntjac were old when other deer were "sharing ancestors with the giraffe".

Their size and habitat make them right for Steep Holm. Whereas most deer are happy with a field of long grass, or a farmer's corn, these are not grazing animals. They are exclusively a browsing deer and spend almost all their time in dense scrub, "an empty ecological niche", as Dansie put it. The island at present has 17 acres of privet and bramble scrub and this area has expanded from a mere six acres in 1950. Nothing has yet held this trend in check.

Visually, they are also right for the island, as they are pocket-size deer blending immediately into the background, and moving around as individuals rather than herds. Their presence on Steep Holm equates with the use by the Normans of islands as naturally contained enclosures for their rabbits. "I have only moved deer that would otherwise be eliminated by shotgun drives," Dr Dansie explains. "But never to places where they might escape and become a problem, albeit an imaginary one."

From the scientific viewpoint, the Steep Holm experiment may be revealing and provide data about the animals' life and habits. This is important as Muntjac is potentially, on present evidence, the most adaptable foreign deer ever to escape into the British countryside. Since a few broke out of parks at Woburn Abbey and Whipsnade in the 1940s the species has established substantial numbers in the south Midlands and westwards to Wales, but its notable achievement is the capacity to thrive in patches of farmland abandoned for ultimate development beside the fringes of London and the new towns of Hertfordshire.

Dr Dansie said: "Many people like to see Muntjac about and it is the large neglected garden that maintains the population in the towns. With their base secure they can wander the streets, grazing the verges, pruning the roses, and gathering acorns under the remaining mature oaks."

In a century it is likely the Muntjac will be known to the suburban inhabitants of every town in England and Wales, though usually as a result of the inevitable road casualties that are the penalty for a species adapting into man's unintended town-edge wildernesses.

Pointers for further research were set out by the Mammal Society of the British Isles in 1959: "Study the acclimatisation of Muntjac. There is some evidence that mortality during hard winters is selective. Are the winter breeding strains being eliminated?" On an island, with its milder winters, the original all-year breeding genes are unlikely to be impaired, though there is no proof this is happening on the mainland anyway.

Jim Taylor Page, compiling the *Field Guide to British Deer*, produced page charts of the seasonal behaviour of each species, except Muntjac. In its place he wrote: "Little is known of the seasonal behaviour of Muntjac in Great Britain. This page is left blank and it is hoped that you will assist in filling it in."

The advantage an island offers for study is a detached and simplified environment. Attention is focused on details that would be difficult to isolate on the mainland. It is difficult to explain quite the significance some trivial event can have on an island, and the excitement it brings to those working there, though the story of explorers Buxton and Hopkins of the arrival of the human flea on a Pacific island does illustrate the curiosity that is the pre-requisite for all research: "The placid natives of Aitutaki, observing that the little creatures were constantly restless and inquisitive, and even at times irritating, drew the reasonable inference that they were the souls of deceased white men."

On summertime trips we hoped to be able to show off the island's strange deer to visitors, though as they have remained few and secretive this cannot be taken as a guarantee. These deer leave few traces of their presence and movement, noticeable paths through the undergrowth only occurring on Steep Holm in early summer in the great tracts of quick-growing, fleshy Alexanders. Slots are only likely to be found in damp soil. Droppings are added regularly to small heaps, often in impenetrable thickets. These unobtrusive qualities are the key to the Muntjac's twentieth century English acceptability, in contrast to the treatment of gregarious species. As Dansie said: "There is no herding or flocking animal whose numbers have not suffered. Is this, perhaps, because man is the supreme visual hunter and as soon as any animal is out of sight is it out of mind? Environment has changed quicker than evolution, and it so happens the Muntjac have also stepped into an empty niche in man's empty and idle mind." You are more likely to see them on television as they have proved very popular with the media. One en-route for Cotswold Wildlife Park featured on the BBC local news from Bristol on 2 March 1977.

As for the wider ecological ethics, I have always tried to prevent the use of any form of herbicide on the island, not so much because of likely ineffectiveness but because I had years of condemning Dorset farmers for spraying and fertilizing their flora out of existence. A report on ecologically-sound defoliants that caught John Fowles's eye "in the dentist's the other day", in 1977, outlined research carried out to eliminate "the ranker weeds" on a single spring application of the growth regulator maleic hydrazide (MH) mixed with the herbicide 2, 4- dichlorophenoxyaceticacid (2, 4-D) which apparently leaves a "low grassy sward" with a "rich variety of plant species". I still think that on Steep Holm it would leave either Alexanders or a desert, but the formula seemed worth recording in case chemicals have to be tried out of utter desperation. Then John Percival ruled it out completely: "This is Dioxin based!"

For all our purist attitudes on agricultural chemicals I continued to be pilloried for my introduction of the Muntjac. "Rodney's wretched pets," John Fowles called them. None was seen on the island throughout that spring and Dr Ernest Neal said he thought they were unlikely to succeed. Michael Yesson teamed up with a gamekeeper to tramp through much of the eastern thickets of bramble and privet for a whole day. They saw and heard nothing, and found no deer-slots or droppings, and so pronounced them to be extinct. "Won't they fall off the island?" Mandy Allsop had asked. I began to think she might be right – she would be, but that's later in the story. Misadventure, in cliff-falls, is the commonest cause of Muntjac deaths.

John Fowles asked on 25 May 1977 for my confession regarding the island's other recently introduced species of mammal:

"Now, Rodney, one last thing that didn't get brought up at the meeting, because I vetoed it privately beforehand with Ernest N. and Tony P. The hedgehogs. They've both been asking around, and can find no one who recalls any previous record of the beasts on the island. Neither of them objects in any way to their presence now on the island, but they both feel they'd keep an even warmer place in their hearts for you if you would come clean on numbers and dates. I promise there will be no repercussions, only their scientific consciences appeased. It's just getting the record straight, and erasing a doubt from all our minds." (Six; May 1975 – released in the smallest room in the Farmhouse ruin which has since been dug out by Jenny Smith and found to be its water-tank.)

It had obviously slipped his mind that he was not only told about their imminent arrival, in April 1975, but had advised me to consider their hibernation and water needs.

The Bruton meeting of 1973, the one at which it was agreed to put a working donkey on to the island, had also accepted my suggestion of introducing hedgehogs. It had rather naively decided upon "a test number" without perhaps giving much thought to the implications of the specimens achieving a natural increase. Despite the fact that the hedgehogs were at least semi-authorised refugees I did not give Bristol Naturalists' Society the pleasure of knowing that anyone else was partially responsible. I was protective of our chairman; he was spared almost all the routine dilemmas and moans inherent in running an inconveniently sited piece of land. When the complainants did find the Belmont House address he was in turn supportive of me. "Goodbye and good riddance" he wrote after one lady had terminated her £5 a year.

He was even less pleased if they phoned. "I wish a special kind of hell upon those who abuse the telephone," he said. The phobia would in time catch up with me; the aversion started when potential island visitors invariably timed their calls to coincide with the evening meal or the onset of sleep. One excuse was logical: "I left phoning till late, so that you'd be home."

Although the Muntjac were released on the island early in 1977, and despite several hundred people visiting the island including some who tramped the undergrowth looking for them, none was seen until 5 July. Then, at 10.00 pm, Howell Jones disturbed a 9-inch high mammal "of indeterminate colour" on an old Nissen hut footing north-west of the Barracks: "It disappeared up the path at very high speed." The following night, at 10.55 pm, Amy Pluim-Mentz saw "a hind leg disappearing into bushes" between Garden Battery and the Barracks. Stan Rendell, on Saturday 23 July at 9.30 pm, met a Muntjac on an overgrown path near a water-hole: "I suddenly saw this brown animal right in front of me. It disappeared into the bushes straight away. I think it had just gone down to get a drink." A few days later at two o'clock one afternoon, a Muntjac burst a hole two feet wide through one of the nets Tony Parsons was using to catch birds. They had bred, as sets of tiny tracks were found running alongside normal sized ones.

July 1977 was, for me, almost daily Steep Holm. It disrupted my business and was now my complete life. I told the Trust's council that they had to find another warden. John Fowles wrote to me on 25 August 1977, telling me Betty Allsop was "guilt-stricken about the burden we are putting on you" but that they feared the unknown of appointing a replacement. As Rab Butler said: "He's the best Prime Minister we've got." That double-edged witticism was hardly adequate for the occasion, not that anything could have saved Sir Anthony Eden after Suez.

John Fowles went on to outline an alternative to resignation. "She did come up with an idea: that you might feel more able to carry on next year if we made you the salaried warden. 'I'd much rather pay Rodney instead of someone, etc' ... I said I thought the essence of the cost for you was time rather than money – but would it make it more bearable?"

It did, for part-time island going and secretarial assistance, to the extent of £115 in 1978, though it would be at £1,560 ten years later.

There was a continuing flow of invective about the introduction of hedgehogs to Steep Holm. In order to protect other members of the committee it had – as was true with the deer – to be presented as my "unauthorised" action. Tony Parsons, as the collector of our natural history data, inevitably took most of the flak. No one wrote directly to me, or I would be quoting their words here, but as with cowards of all ages they put their pressure on those who were innocent. Dr Ernest Neal was on the Trust's council. He was deeply upset that people might think him to be involved. John Fowles placated them, up to a point; that he would rein-in his maverick warden, and wrote to me on 17 October 1977:

"Tony will doubtless let us see the Bristol Naturalists' report on the island. I gather he's already scotched the idea that de-hedgehogging the place is feasible. I imagine, even if they aren't eating the eggs, that their nocturnal ramblings must be causing some of the gulls to desert. We shall know next year, I hope."

By the end of 1977 another schism, with Friends of the Earth, was no longer even a memory at their London offices. The accountant there wrote to John Fowles: "I have noticed that we have some bank statements for the Kenneth Allsop Memorial Fund and am concerned about the control of the fund. ERR, our charity research arm, tell me that they are not sure whom the fund has passed to, but have given me your name and address."

One grandiose aberration which I failed to foist upon the island in 1978 was a plan to combat dereliction at the Barracks and achieve the re-building of the farmhouse, two eastern cottages and Inn. I had suggested they were turned into multiple units of holiday accommodation along the lines of the Landmark Trust properties to make Steep Holm a mini-Lundy. Sadly, to make it viable, it would probably have needed something extra in the form of at least one row of holiday chalets, and that kind of development on the island was anathema, and covenant-breaking.

The deciding impracticality, as John Fowles put it, was "the actual high-inaccessibility problem". Costs then, he considered, were "at the very minimum £100,000" and he calculated that with ten units bringing in a total of £10,000 "even then, by the time you deduct our upkeep and servicing and having to pay someone to be full-time on the island, it must still smell like a poor return on investment".

I had found a Cheltenham businessman who seemed prepared to take the gamble, though his immediate impetus was a piece of complete misinformation. He quoted someone from the Meteorological Office as saying that weather conditions would make it impossible to sail to Steep Holm on only five days a year. On those, he said, it would be economic to fly the punters in by helicopter from Weston or Lulsgate. We were enjoying the comforts of Geoffrey Taylor's Holbrook House Hotel, in sheltered south Somerset, and it seemed impolite to demolish my host's cherished illusions by pointing out that there were often times when it was not possible to get a boat to Steep Holm for five days in a week.

We parted with the outline of a scheme that could have made Steep Holm into a miniature Portmeirion, the Italianate Welsh holiday village designed by Sir Clough Williams-Ellis. The dream was for a few Laura Ashley interiors and a return to real architecture at a time when I wanted to crucify the Labour councillors who had rehoused their electorates in rabbit hutches in the sky. The Steep Holm of 1978 was also very different from the island of 1988. There was still wartime dereliction and we were all exhausted from the clearance of the piles of debris that we had inherited, across the perimeter path and beside, above and actually inside the vital reservoir at the back of the Barracks. Steep Holm was then a world away from being paradise.

The "grand scheme" evaporated into the reality of a decade of do-it-yourself as the saving of the island's architecture became an endless holding operation. Doug Tripp and his family of builders, helped by Ken Thorne, gave the Barracks slates a remedial coating and inside Chris Maslen and Jenny Smith spent the summer of 1982 tearing down the weighty and collapsing lime ceilings to reveal the majesty of a timbered roof on the scale of a mediaeval long-house. The walls did not quite make Laura Ashley standards but they went a classy Wedgwood blue.

Less was achieved with the ruins. Consolidation at the Farmhouse was over-done with mortar that caps the walls like icing on a Christmas cake. My own minor contribution at the Tenement was to underpin a crumbling corner. As for the Priory ruin the mediaeval walls require lime-mortar pointing. Cliff Cottage remains a single decaying wall. Only at the Inn has the semblance of a building arisen out of the mound of stone rubble that 930 Port Construction and Repair Company of the Royal

Engineers had reduced it to in July 1941. The plan for its long-term restoration, though this time into a two-storey rather than a three-storey building, was drawn up by Bere Regis architect Fred Pitfield. The stones go back on the wall as and when I am there to climb on top and can persuade Chris Maslen to pass me rocks. Equally important are the lads who have been coerced into mixing my Walcrete; at the time of writing they are Glenn Weatley and Justin Burt from Burnham-on-Sea.

Cliff-climbing to replant the Wild Leeks has led to a proliferation of clumps but it was only off the island that we were able to achieve anything similar for the Wild Peony. It did at least give me a chance to send out a press release: "International author saves Britain's rarest plant." The publicity "for which I don't exactly bless you" included "a ludicrously inexact piece about the island" in his own Lyme Regis News.

The experts at Kew Gardens found great difficulty in persuading the seeds of the Steep Holm Wild Peony to germinate. They did not respond to the various clinical and chemical short-cuts that were intended to start the process. Unlike the seed of which I was unaware, either that it was inside my sodden Wellington boot, or that it had then slipped into the crack between two flagstones in the foundation of my hillside cottage in Somerset. There it now grows and flowers, its yearly gardening being to chip away a bit more stone and concrete.

John Fowles did his growing on another southern slope, at the seaside, in what I dubbed the Belmont Botanical Garden. It stretches above the Cobb harbour at Lyme Regis. He wrote to tell me of his mega-success on 31 March 1979: "As of about one week ago, I am now some six dozen peony seedlings 'richer' than I was before, all from the 1976 batch of about 120 planted – seedlings are still coming so the count may be higher – certainly higher than the rather pessimistic Kew germination percentage, anyway.

"I had clear evidence this time of another early hazard they suffer from – pecking by birds when their arched first-stem necks poke into daylight. At least a dozen had been bitten off or pulled out entire. One can hardly blame the birds, they look very wormlike at this stage in shape and deep pink colour. I've hastily wired the bed over, needless to say. But I suspect this may be a not negligible factor in natural reproduction on the island. The culprits here are probably blackbirds and robins – of the latter I had direct evidence while I was working on the bed, as a robin came and had a dig at a seedling only four feet away from me. The seedlings are so bright-coloured that they might well attract gull-attention on the island, too."

He added that plants from early batches were also showing. From that time there has been a steady re-introduction of mainland-germinated Wild Peonies to the island with mixed results. Gardened by Stan and Joan Rendell, and their team of weeders, they have flourished once again beside the Priory ruins. Planted by me on the most precipitous ledges of the eastern cliffs they have succumbed either to direct bird-attack or the chicken-run conditions that the gulls create.

I have had, over the years, more letters about the Wild Peony than any other subject. Another has come as I write this, from Mrs Jessica M. Dean of Colliton at Porlock, who writes:

"Thank you for the news about Steep Holm. When I was last there about 30 or 40 years ago it was horrible. Narrow paths through Alexanders plants and privet. We were dive-bombed by screaming gulls and could not avoid stepping on their eggs. The only peace was sitting on the gun emplacements among the rusty barbed wire. We were not allowed near the Peony corner. When I asked if I might have seed I was treated like a felon or worse, and one of the party stood up for me and said I only wanted to propagate it. Now I am sure it is all different under your management."

Partially, in that we dealt with the barbed wire, and the gull population subsequently crashed to numbers which we regard as acceptable. Others, however, are still not impressed and at the annual meeting of the Trust in Weston on 1 August 1987, for the first time since we had taken over the island, I admitted that we do have adverse consumer reaction. Extracts were read out at some length on HTV's evening news on the Monday and there was an interview broadcast with Radio Bristol. The press enjoyed the castigation of "Moaning Minnies". I called it an overdue exercise in glasnost and intended the comments to spotlight conservation dilemmas on Steep Holm and the impossibility of pleasing everyone. Drawing attention to the letters of complaint succeeded in pleasing no one.

All begin the same: "Dear Sir stroke Madam." Then they fall into two categories. Extreme west wing or extreme east wing. West wing views are those of nature and green living. East wing views are from cosy suburbia. The first come on re-cycled paper. The second on Basildon Bond.

I gave an example of each, but only with extracts because what they do have in common is that they are long – very long.

The first writer is male:

"The first thing that struck me" – about the island – "were the cups being handed out with the cold drinks. Disposable ones made of a synthetic thermoplastic material which has long been established to cause destruction of the ozone. Not only when such cups are disposed of are they damaging to the environment but pollution of some sort is also caused during the fabrication of thermoplastics. Add to this of course that such materials are using up valuable finite resources during their production.

"The cost in monetary terms when purchasing such cups might be cheap, but when measured in other terms it is far greater indeed. I saw other small things out of place, there was another type of disposable plastic cup, I believe for the tea, also normal cleaning materials, washing-up liquid etc. These pollute the water. Non polluting bio-degradable cleaning materials are available.

"While in the Barracks I pointed out these contradictions to somebody who was working there selling pamphlets and stamps. He agreed with my observation" – sensible chap – "but stated that it was for convenience that such cups were in use. Your convenience, unfortunately, that is partly destroying our planet, and anyway would washing a few dishes be so inconvenient?"

His case is unanswerable. The solution might seem to be to keep Steep Holm inviolate as the uninhabited rock that nature intended. Unfortunately, however, human beings cannot be disinvented, and neither can the boat, and those who spend occasional hours on the island would be free to go in search of other wild places and inflict their pollution, or pollution by proxy, on another corner of this abused planet.

At least we can understand the inherent contradictions. Yet his argument is not a concept that the east wing faction would consider for a moment. Suburbanism is epitomised by the lady who came into the Barracks and swept past the basic but cheerful catering arrangements and out the other door, proclaiming "Disgusting – and to think that it is owned by the National Trust!"

They, you will remember, turned down the chance of having the island on the grounds of "insurmountable access difficulties". There have been times when we would all agree with them. What they have done for all pieces of cherished land is to bring the values of middle class respectability for the benefit of a clique who visualise their armchair countryside as an extension to the grounds of the Park Lane Hilton. Let another lady articulate their case:

"Dear Sir stroke Madam.

I have recently spent a very disappointing day trip to Steep Holm. It was very upsetting to land on the island beach and see numerous dead adult and baby seagulls. Some looked like they had been there quite a long time."

Death does tend to restrict mobility.

"We planned to see the island by following the nature trail but the paths were so badly overgrown, often waist-high in nettles and brambles. It was a most unpleasant walk.

"There were no seating facilities at all provided, and it was terrible to see the amount of litter – mainly tin cans and bottles thrown on the ground. I am sure it would help if waste-bins were provided.

"I realise all the work on the island is carried out by volunteers, but surely ... "

It ends there, because I have lost the following pages.

In this case the harrowing finale was to return to the island's beach for the trip back and to find that yet another young gull was in a distressing condition.

Perhaps we should have an extra sign: "Wildlife is asked to desist from dying on the island."

As for other aspects of the description I wonder if we are talking about the same island.

Anyway, I have tried to fairly represent samples of two conflicting viewpoints that are irreconcilable.

Part of our clientele comes out of a sense of adventure and delights in a ferocious voyage. They want the isle of desolation that we found in 1973 when the only catering facility was the Thermos flask and often that went home shattered as a casualty of the hostile environment.

At the opposite pole are those who shudder from the moment they see our landing plank, the steps off the beach, rutted path surfaces, and have their first encounter with the island's resilient flora. Their shaking progresses into hysterical convulsions as they are swooped upon by an irate herring gull. Not all the wildlife has got round to dying.

Perhaps the answer is indifference. We need to accept that we are not primarily concerned with people. That the island is still a wild place, with wild inhabitants. Human intrusion is to be tolerated at the edges, and as onlookers rather than policemen. It is our task to help the island to regain its natural beauty but not to convert it into something that meets all human expectations.

The achievement is that we have transformed it from a tangle of war debris into a half-way natural mess. It is no longer a tip but it does have a certain resemblance to an offshore overgrown garden.

Even to maintain that is at the cost of continuing human endeavour. Here we are also out of line with society's general modern ways. Only at the fringes, for less than ten percent of our financial turnover, have we been the grateful recipients of government and local authority funding.

If we are to submit our "Dear Sir stroke Madam" letter to Number 10 Downing Street it is to point out that despite espousing the self-help Victorian work ethic we have become the poor relation of the other mid Bristol Channel island. That has money poured into it from Wales – which is their concern – and London – which is ours.

I resent having to claw at a rockface with a bucket of cement, almost unaided now that we attract so few volunteers for Victorian doses of hard labour. Or rather I resent that as I do so a red helicopter is droning over Flat Holm, for what seemed like hours, bringing and dropping objects that could be no heavier than things we have struggled to man-handle up our far more precipitous cliffs. One lift, I was told, was for the departing lighthousemen of Trinity House – replaced by automation – but as the delivery in question was a Klargester septic-tank it seemed strangely timed.

Flat Holm investment from the public purse must be nearer to half a million than it is to our total public input, over eighteen years, of only £20,000. Their example is of what you can do in a short time if you throw money at a problem.

Ours are the frustrations of getting there, one day perhaps, after winning through in the yearly repeats of the battle for self-sufficiency. The sad thing is that we live in a society that is so conditioned by the big-spend that it does not believe there can be anywhere doing things differently.

'Rodney's wretched pets': one of, to use John Fowles's expression. A fleeting glimpse of a Muntjac crossing the carpet of young Alexanders beside the Barracks. Seen from the north-west. Photographed by John Pitfield on 5 December 1991.

Village pump: Ken Cass having plumbed and primed a cast-iron Victorian hand-pump above the reservoir behind the Barracks. It is 1.36 metres high and was made in Devon by 'PLUMPTON & SON, CULLOMPTON'. Seen from the south-west. Photographed by Mary Cass in 1986.

Years of hard labour

The island can absorb any amount of physical labour and generally there is little by way of visible change to show for it. Neither will the words be much by way of consolation, for most tasks have a transient usefulness which is far short of even the limited human span. The notable achievements are the bursts of progress that leave improvements which we recognise, and usually take for granted on the mainland, but thereon come the silent maintenance, and for that there is never recognition or thanks.

In July 1975, for the first time since the Second World War, there was running water on Steep Holm. A 600 gallon tank had been raised to the top of the Barracks roof and piping fitted to connect the underground reservoir with the kitchen. This was carried out over four days by Yeovil engineer Michael Yesson, aided by his first wife, Pauline, with Gay Meyrick and members of the Axbridge Caving Group. The materials were either donated by Mr Yesson, or otherwise salvaged by him from amongst the wartime debris that was still lying all over the island. The group also tackled the filthy job of unblocking lavatories with the almost equally obnoxious assistance of bottles of hydrochloric acid. Apart from doing all this for the island, the volunteers paid their own boat fares and took their own food, so no cost whatever fell upon the Allsop Trust funds.

The central section of the Barracks was then derelict and its whitewashing was achieved by a team of Girl Guides, led by Mrs Joyce Phillips, from Weston-super-Mare. Despite our attention to its leaks the rear window had decayed beyond repair and I asked Richard Tripp to brick it up. This seemed a desperate remedy, but it faced north and let in virtually no light, and his brickwork is smart and seems to give the room more depth.

This work was being carried out so that the Barracks could house those who would transform the island. Our own volunteers were scavenging like gypsies, or the Ukranians I once watched clearing Studland Heath of its explosive wartime debris as their chosen alternative to a reunion with Joseph Stalin; but there was more to be done than the endless collection of scrap metal. We never found any Ukrainians, nor on the top of the island the unexploded ammunition they were so carefree in collecting, but we soon had nine young men and women from France and Germany. They were led by John Cockings, on behalf of the International Voluntary Service, and for a fortnight of the 1975 drought they sweltered at Split Rock Battery and peeled off its covering of Second World War detritus to reveal the Palmerstonian double gun battery which had been scheduled as an ancient monument.

There was a hitch over their food. I was told they were bringing food; and they were told food was being provided. There was a desperate rush to find something, which in the end was plentiful and varied if a little un-English. It included 84 lbs of cling peaches, a sack of spaghetti, and a catering pack of curry powder.

They supplemented it from the island. One lad slung beach pebbles 90 feet with perfect precision and there was at least one experiment with sweet and sour Herring Gull. The French boys constructed a glass cage which they filled with snails, keeping them there "to clear their bodies", and at the end of the fortnight I liberated the uneaten specimens.

There was some publicity for the operation but it was not wholly welcomed. I did my best to justify the first major work by a Trust in the name of Kenneth Allsop, going into the preservation of a military monument: "It is as much part of the island's life as the birds, so we have adapted our plans to make room for some huge guns." One lady was unconvinced: "Enclosed is my donation towards your effort, but I think it is a pity about the guns!"

On 28 September 1975 I reported: "Steep Holm now looks far less of a rubbish dump than it did in July. Work projects have continued and the main impact has been made by Eric Reid from Kent. He has been supported by Michael Yesson, Rodney Freeman, David Reid, Tony Parsons, David Lindley and a team from Sidcot School."

They had turned the Barracks into a functioning building that was most weeks home for three or four staying visitors who had come in response to a small-ad for "spartan self-catering island weeks" in the satirical magazine Private Eye. These were a success because of the amazing weather, a flat sea and searing heat, and the boatmen kept reminding me that we would not be getting away with such a complex timetable of comings and goings in a normal year. The advertisements were then inserted into a series of ornithological and conservation journals and found only two takers in total.

Private Eye readers also turned out to be more self-sufficient and resourceful which, we were finding, were essential qualities for becoming a successful islander. Sidcot School provided some enthusiastic boys and I directed them into Garden Battery, the Victorian western barbette of which was covered to the

66

rim and overflowing down the cliff with soil and rock that had been displaced in 1941 when the concrete emplacement for a 6-inch naval gun was built beside it. To their excitement, and mine, they reached the top of an up-ended Georgian C-pivot cannon that was still in situ in the 1866-68 Palmerstonian fortifications.

There were to be two subsequent rediscoveries of the island's military archaeology that resulted from my inspired guesses. These were the finding and digging out of the underground magazine at Summit Battery West and the location and exposure of the ninth Victorian gun barrel beneath the Battery Observation Post which had been built on top of it at Rudder Rock in 1941. On the other hand, my failed hunches wasted hundreds of work hours in the heat of 1975-76, as the teams of boys and girls dug deep into the ground at Garden Battery in search of its magazines and the island's other lost Victorian cannon and its Georgian pivot-barrel that supported the carriage.

The 1975 drought is not the remembered one – that was the megascorcher of the century in the following summer – but its end in September had been dramatic. One of my most hairy cliffside operations was above the eastern beach where the intensity of the summer heat had expanded the stones off their dirt-bed footings. They remained safe until the heat ended and contraction set in. Many were tottering above the cliff path. I record the phenomenon in the Trust's first minutebook: "Some weighed a hundredweight and crashed down at a touch. They were finally levered into the sea. The gales and rain battered this corner of the island and at one stage stones were dropping on to the path of their own accord at the rate of about one a minute."

Messy jobs continued. On the Barracks roof it was 150 litres of Synthaproof, which is liquid tar. Off the island it was a writ in Weston-super-Mare county court which found in the Trust's favour and awarded £95 in settlement and about £25 costs arising from charity events which had been held in our name.

Despite many requests the cash had not been handed over, so I went to law, with the strong support of television pundit Anthony Smith, and a determined letter from Richard Mabey: "There are an increasing number of cases of the misuse of money for charities that are giving the whole fund-raising business a bad public image. I think we have a duty to try and turn the tide a little, even though it may cost us more than we would like."

Tony Parsons was now coming to my support on the island. In the heat of 1975 it was plain sailing, to a record fifteen Saturdays in succession, and it was to my relief that Tony stepped aboard to take three Sunday trips.

At the other end they had to contend with the jagged obstacle that was once the ladder from the beach on to the quay wall. Michael Yesson had to suspend all his other work projects after the winter of 1975-76 when gales tore away the remains of the ladder. His replacement wide-tread metal ladder would suffer the same fate and its successor would be a flight of wooden steps constructed by ex-BOAC radio engineer Ken Cass who had retired to Burnham-on-Sea and took over Michael's work when the latter was preoccupied on the mainland with a change of marriage partners.

Forest School Camps came for a fortnight to carry on the enhancement process that was converting the island from a tip into something that was visually presentable. They and the returnees from the previous summer found the 1976 temperatures were set to break the 1975 records. Rubble removal and clearance of collapsed Nissen huts went on throughout the tropical summer. Groups of boys and girls were provided by Sidcot School, Weston Rangers, Wrington Rangers, Bath Rangers, Long Ashton Rangers, Weston Sea Cadets and our own crèche of youngsters which Colin Graham and I had gathered around us in the former Railway Inn at Milborne Port.

My only panics on the island were the fear of the arrival of the national problem. Dorset was burning for weeks and the pine smoke, which would normally have delighted the senses, was coming deep into Somerset on the southerly breeze. Steep Holm was set to burn when I found it was a Guiding imperative to have a good bonfire. I tried to restrict them to the concrete beside the Barracks but despite the television coverage of the heath fires, and now the burning forests in Wales, they had no comprehension of the inferno that could grip a tinderbox island. As the undergrowth was cleared from around and inside the ruins I grasped for ecological straws when the logical argument failed. "Pile the cut trees on to the nearby brambles to thicken them into dense bushes," I urged. "That will provide more scrub cover and nesting sites for the birds."

It was on 29 September 1976 that I condemned the plaster of the Barracks ceiling to the dustbin of history though the tortuous process of improving that immense building would take its toll on the energies of Doug Tripp, his sons Stephen and Richard, Ken Thorne, Mike Parker, Tony Wilson, and finally taken to its present glory in the summer of 1982 by Chris Maslen and Jenny Smith, an ex-Wrington Vale Ranger who has been returning to the island since 1976.

My memo about the Barracks ceiling seems so simple in foresight but utterly lacks any realisation of the difficulties and mess that would come down with the tons of displaced plaster: "Swanage Railway Station is a Victorian building in a state of neglect and structurally very similar to the Barracks. Like ours, it is a single storey with a very high roof laid on a total covering of wood. Their solution has been to repair the roof and then remove the ceiling.

"This exposes the underside of the wood and it can then be tackled and made good. Finally the entire woodwork is saturated with preservative. The finished 'hall' takes on the appearance of a mediaeval church and is not draughty either as the total sealing of the roof renders any ceiling unnecessary. The advantage, apart from looks, is that you don't have a ceiling to repair."

It all sounded so easy, and it was for me, as I did nothing to bring it about. The demise of the ceiling was as much due to natural decay. If Isaac Newton had lived in a house like this he would never have needed to go outdoors for inspiration. Weekly there was another section of crumbled lime scattered across the floor. Ultimately, the double-dosing of the impressive and exposed woodwork would be forced on us by a constant trickle of sawdust, coming down as a fine mist, from a billion woodworm. The "us" in this case was Ken Cass, who twice went the whole length of the main hall in a slow progress on a tower scaffold with the paraphernalia of chemical warfare.

That was, by far, the worst job anyone has ever tackled on the island during Europe's decades of peace. Being saturated with those toxins would have killed off a lesser mortal but Ken Cass was going to be working on the island into his eighties. So perhaps the chemicals are truly preservative. To me, however, they are a thousand times more noxious than the filth in the reservoir filter-beds and the sequel to the cry: "The toilets are blocked again!" Those organic problems I do attend to, but I try to avoid the carcinogens.

Ken Cass also made the display cabinets in the Barracks which finished off the decor. The shop counter provided by Doug Tripp, and serviced by his first wife, Audrey, has now been complemented by a larger display, constructed by Chris Maslen and Anton Dubois, which was manned for many years by Mary Cass and Ann Pike.

Audrey Tripp was enthralled by the island and continued to come and mother its volunteers and visitors until cancer cruelly confined her to bed and then hospital. Her ashes are buried at Summit Battery.

Mary Cass became our second tea-lady and has had only a short mainland grounding whilst nursing a broken ankle which she suffered on Steep Holm service at Anchor Head slipway. She mothers the visitors with similar attention and cheerfulness as husband Ken tinkers away in the back-room on the latest modification to one of the water-pumps or the plumbing. His achievement was to restore a Victorian village pump, cast at Cullompton foundry, which I found in an antique shop. It is the emergency hand-operated alternative to the petrol-driven mechanical system.

There is also a lot of Ken Cass handiwork visible around the island's beach. The gated fortifications are to deter unautho-rised landers who have done such damage to the island and will probably eventually score a fatal own-goal in a misadventure against themselves.

Ken Cass must also have the credit for our one great frivolity and the best adventure in the life and times of Allsop Island.

One of the island's Georgian C-pivot guns, displaced from the east barbette of Summit Battery, lay behind the Second World War 6-inch gun emplacement there until 25 September 1986, when it was lifted by Lieutenant Jerry Spence's Sea King of 707 Naval Air Squadron, Yeovilton, and carried from obscurity to become the military showpiece outside the Barracks. It is a cast-iron smooth-bore 24-pounder of the Napoleonic period, dated about 1798, and ten feet long. Similar guns were placed at the top of Martello towers. The left trunnion carries the maker's initials "W Co" – standing for Walker and Company of Rother-ham, Ironfounders to the Board of Ordnance – and on the right trunnion the number 229. This gun has a 6⅛-inch bore and fired a muzzle-loaded cannon ball. The guns aboard HMS *Victory* are also Walker cannon.

Though they were never fired on Steep Holm in the nine-teenth century, being there only to be set into the ground as pivots for the later guns, the Barracks cannon has since smelt gunpowder. As the Navy lads unleashed its harness, and the gun jolted on to the wooden carriage that Ken Cass had con-structed, a dummy shell was produced. John Pitfield proceeded to stuff the breech of the gun with black powder and then pushed padding around the shell. Only Ken Cass seemed to take the old fashioned explosive seriously and asked if it was really worth the risk of blowing apart both the gun and the carriage. Stan and Joan Rendell were oblivious to the contribution that gunpowder has made to the butcher's bill of history. They and some of the television cameramen had to be firmly dissuaded from a closer look as John Pitfield announced his countdown.

Georgian firepower was superbly demonstrated with a textbook bang that might have won John an admiring wink from Nelson himself. An exceedingly loud explosion cleared out the dirt and debris from the barrel and hurtled the wooden shell in a perfect trajectory seawards, half a mile due south in an assault on "Chernobyl" – the island has a broadside view of Hinkley Point nuclear power station – and John Watts turned the *Weston Lady* on a successful pursuit of the projectile.

That gorgeous Bonfire Night smell of used fireworks, complemented by the claret of one's second childhood, clung to the gun as the Navy departed in style. I jumped up and down on the barrel as the Sea Kings – two in number so that one could film the other – zoomed in to give us a victory salute. It was a close fly-past with landing lights on. Excitement exacts its price; never has the island seemed so boring as on the following trip. Neither helicopters nor cannon fire nor anything else to play with. It is, perhaps, not good to indulge in perfect days.

Having the odd film crew aboard is nothing out of the ordinary. John Hurt, the actor, came to Steep Holm in June 1976 for the making of *The Island* which was a 40 minute horror film produced by HTV in a series entitled "Classics Dark and Dangerous". Later, for a longer load of hocum there were breathtaking helicopter runs at the cliffs, dummies tossed into the sea, and Richard Tripp poised on the rocks as an extra. Richard could only be seen from a distance because it was an Indian film and they were short of Asians, but they disguised him well. I am told the title of the epic was the Hindi word for "Flame" and that it ended with the destruction of the island, James Bond style, with the conflagration of a large model of Steep Holm that had been made in the studios back in Bombay. I spotted garish posters for the finished film in Stepney's Commercial Road but regretfully never stopped to search out the ethnic cinema that was showing it.

As for the island itself, and its fulltime inhabitants, their time was to come in Simon King's film story of the life and misfortunes of *Herrag the Herring Gull*. Most of this delightful saga, which included footage of the island's Peregrine falcons and the Muntjac deer, was based on the Herring Gull's birth and his adolescence before leaving Bristol Channel. Simon King made regular visits to the island but seldom had to fall back on his contrived story lines, as nature provided better. The most dramatic intervention, only the less harrowing section of which was included in the finished film, showed a predatory Greater Black-backed Gull taking and repeatedly dropping and then picking up again an unfortunate Herring Gull chick. This was the major British wildlife film for the Christmas of 1986.

Having film crews on the island is always an adventure into the unexpected. The less intrepid soon realise that cliff paths are incompatible with the conveyance of state-of-the-art equipment. "It's worth £30,000" they warn as they reluctantly accept your offer to carry the camera after you notice they have started to sway. On the bad days it will degenerate into Scotch and cards in the Barracks. The best times, however, are when it goes the other way into pure camp theatre. At the end of one day I raised my hands to be stripped of the radio microphone lead. My thanks were returned with interest: "Not at all, the pleasure was all mine!" It is sometimes good for the ego to return for a few hours to the cosmopolitan culture that is usually a million miles away from life on a rock.

Though we like to feel that we have adjusted to spells of island living, one is sometimes upstaged when a visitor goes native. In 1986, Rosemary Mackinlay from Infafa Beach, South Africa, defied the rocks and stinging nettles to become the first person known to have made a thorough exploration of the island bare-footed.

The reality of ordinary days is that we fuss with yet more supplies for basic needs or practical refinements which we all take for granted in our mainland homes. One of the heaviest delivery trips was a boat-load of five tonnes of concrete blocks with which Mike Prangle would construct the outdoor toilet block at the Barracks. We had trouble getting them ashore until I remembered the wartime methods of the 1941 advance party of Royal Engineers. They unloaded into the sea and picked everything up as the tide ebbed.

Less pleasant to bring ashore, on arrival at South Landing, was the boat full of asbestos roofing sheets for the east end of the Barracks. That was then open to the air. The sheets had been provided by Ernest Paniccia, a huge horse-dealer from Wincanton, who effortlessly loaded them at Knightstone Causeway. John Pitfield and I slipped and struggled to get them on to the rocks – it was a marriage of incompatible shapes – and then up the steps. It was the most exhausting three hours of my life and only residual English reserve prevents me from expressing the extent of the gratification I felt to John for his suffering. The island hardships have been front-line experiences that have solidified friendships for life.

Chris Maslen then had the problem of getting them to the top and it was for his companion, Dave Reid, another push to the limits of human endurance. Chris could make us all seem wimps by coming up the incline from South Landing with a hundredweight of pebbles in his hands and a similar weight of damp sand in a back-pack. And then he would return for more.

For weeks this went on with Mike Prangle completing toilets and Stonehouse chipshop owner Brian Bailey masterminding the complete reroofing of the eastern wing of the Barracks.

When they had turned it into dormitories for the benefit of stranded visitors, the island's only practical insurance policy against the inevitable emergencies, we then had to fit the building out with fifty ex-Navy bunks and mattresses. They were also weighty and painful to bring across and we all carried sections up in the morning when we were still fresh from arrival, but Colin Graham insisted on martyring his back by carrying them long into the afternoon. Between visits I had to drive him into Gloucester for bouts of alternative medicine on his spine. All the Coke and chocolates had to be carried up to the shop. "How do you get it all up here?" is a frequent visitors' question, unless they have been press-ganged into helping.

This went on for years, until Mrs Philippa Bowkett of Burnham-on-Sea visited the island and spent the winter of 1990-91 running an appeal fund to buy a Honda power carrier. She raised over £1,700 to pay for the machine, its garage, and spares. This amazing little truck, on caterpillar tracks, climbs the beach, steps and incline, with up to half a tonne of sand and cement. As for stores, it has been piled high with cases of drink and boxes of chocolate. Chris Maslen had it working virtually non-stop for 50 hours, over a bank holiday weekend. We all wonder how we ever managed without it.

The unsung heroes of the days when the big boats come, the visits of the *Waverley* and the *Balmoral*, have been Terry Gore, Ian Round and Mike Smith who took over from Colin Graham in the strenuous ordeal of wading into the sea to carry the visitors ashore. That is not how it is meant to happen, but theory always falls well short of reality on an island.

For most of the 1980s the intending visitor had to contend with climbing the steps on to the quay. The Ken Cass set of steps were nowhere as awesome as their predecessors but they still had many trembling. At the top was a cage, intended as a safeguard against a misplaced footing, but there was a serious fall. At other times the problem was the sea, literally swilling around the base of the steps, and once Avon Fire Service were on hand to lay ladders so that Joan Rendell could escape from the last island of submerging beach pebbles to the quayside.

The concrete replacements are as safe as steps can be, safer I would say than the stairs in an average house, but they have absorbed their share of preparatory labour. First the pebbles had to be dug out and an engineering project, planned by Chris Maslen, enlisting a battalion of Venture Scouts, built up a series of narrowing platforms. These in turn have changed the general land-form of the beach and heightened its top end. The island off an island from which the firemen plucked Joan Rendell has for a time become a formidable mound of pebbles. Nothing on a beach is permanent, however, and continuity if not blatant repetition is the theme that controls Steep Holm life.

Something similar, though fortunately at an unimportant location in terms of general access, has been happening over the years to the Monks' Well where the island itself keeps slipping to cover the well-head. Wartime soldiers told me about its location and in 1976 I removed a ton of scree – easier than it sounds as I pushed the stones over the cliff – to reveal its armoured steel shutter which is set between railway lines at ground level.

It was an immediate hazard for both visitors and wildlife. One of the former had a bad fall but was saved from the rocks, 13 metres below, by the dense canopy of ivy. Those who did make the expedition frequently left the lid partially open and the casualties from their carelessness included birds and hedgehogs. Doug Tripp gave us a metal fire-escape ladder to help people descend the cliff and Ken Cass erected a safety rail.

In 1986-87 Chris Maslen and Jenny Smith, helped by Philip Dolphin, built a set of steps down to the Monks' Well from a point 50 metres north-west of Cliff Cottage. As for the well itself, the scree slope moves relentlessly to cover it, with an accretion rate that is staggering, but at least that prevents it from being a trap for either hedgehogs or man. This interesting relic has defied all attempts at making it either presentable or idiot-proof. One man told me he had let go the top, thinking it would be held in position by its own weight, and that it had nearly sliced his wife's feet off. For some reason he seemed to consider it was my fault.

That we have had the manpower available over the years to

tackle so much has been primarily because of the relative self-sufficiency that visitors bring us, and the fact that despite some problem trips we do average thirty a year that are pleasingly uneventful, but there have been subsidies from our benefactors. Two have done so much that they must have personal mentions. Frank Harris of Manchester visited the island in the 1920s and at eighty-seven he was still sending me donations and letters of encouragement. Behind in seniority but at eighty-one the most amazing of the island stalwarts is Ken Cass who not only works full days but insists on no reimbursement for much of the materials he has brought us. I won't estimate a value, because that loses all meaning with the passage of a little time, but it would have been enough to put an extension on his bungalow at Burnham. Mike Prangle also kindly forgets to charge for many things, as did Michael Yesson a decade before.

I have always tried to find someone who will pay for my sand and Walcrete and 2,000 pairs of Marigold gloves – the total to date, preferably large-size red but a combination of red and yellow as a mixed pair is fun to tease the continuity girls of our occasional television crews. My principal paymaster of the early 1980s was the Countryside Commission who, through Godfrey Phillips, took a close interest in us, though our adventures sometimes seemed tame when compared with his expeditions to pre-Gorbachev Russia. Somewhat nearer the capitalist system has been Councillor Jim Dickson from Weston-super-Mare who helped win me some more pocket money for mortar and a few payments from Woodspring District Council towards the rest of the workforce's efforts in keeping a roof over the Barracks. Hazel Burns has kept the books since 1978 and faced the worries of the times when nothing came through to make them balance.

The hidden cost behind all this is that we have to pay the ferryman. The only perk for the labour force is that they have an uncharged boat ride but there is no such thing as a free trip. The Allsop Trust has to pay it for them. Our subsidy in this direction, as a general safety-net to meet the multiplicity of incidental expenses, is a regular grant from Woodspring Council. It was always accompanied by the keen interest of their chief executive, Bob Moon, who soon became the island's best friend in local government, and joined the Trust's committee on his retirement in 1990.

Big John: author John Fowles (standing) and warden Rodney Legg on an outcrop at Split Rock, amid the gullery as the island begins to dry off towards the end of the breeding season. Seen from the south. Photographed by Colin Graham in July 1976.

Lost people and property

One of the problems of having people intruding into a wild place is that they tend to get lost. This particularly applies to the Welsh who get disorientated in the voyage to Steep Holm and start identifying Cardiff on the west Somerset coast. Confusion has worrying practical implications in that people can go the wrong way when looking for the beach and the boat home. It can also waste time on arrival as happened in the pre-signs era when ornithologist Tony Parsons first came to Steep Holm and jogged, with a military-weight pack on his back and a bundle of bamboo poles under each arm, around the northern cliffs and did a circuit of three-quarters of the island before he found the Barracks. The compromise between a wilderness and the provision of information were the signs erected by Ken Cass in 1980.

Most would be wiped out by the weather and wind but the second generation of numbers – to key in with *The Steep Holm Guide* – have proved more durable. It is not to belittle Ken's time and effort with those signs to point out that they co-exist uneasily with a rocky environment. John Fowles voiced this concern, and also vetoed a suggestion, frequently made by elderly visitors, for the provision of park benches:

"The one thing I am distinctly not happy about is the idea of having green signs everywhere – I can't see that this is necessary at all, given the detail and goodness of the map. Perhaps names of batteries, but too many I would count as landscape pollution – quite apart from the expense and nuisance of upkeep for us. Nor do I see why trail pointers are needed. The route is totally clear from the map. Pointering and numbering in excess destroys the naturalness and wildness of a place. Please go easy on this side of it."

John Fowles opposed what he regarded as suburbanisation creeping on to the island. He wrote to me on 5 September 1984: "My only quibble is whether seats are necessary, and I loathe the idea of 'municipal' concrete ones. Surely the 'sarcophagus' kind, built of island stone, would be better and least obtrusive." It was not just on Steep Holm that he applied this logic. There was at that time the offer by Dame Elisabeth Frink of a sculpture of a Peregrine in memory of Kenneth Allsop, which the art-in-landscape charity Common Ground had tried to place on Eggardon Hill. The National Trust, the owners there since 1979, were none too happy. Fowles supported them, against the wishes of Ken's widow, he told me on 16 June 1983:

"The Frink thing. As I've told Betty I'm absolutely against having it on Eggardon – as I'm sure Ken himself would have been in his right mind. This is nothing to do with my affection for him, or my (very great) liking for Frink's work. In my view the National Trust are absolutely right to keep such sites 'clean'. It may be Ken and Frink today but the other end of that wedge is Viscount Nobody and some Royal Academy ham."

John Fowles added that in this case he considered "the island is a very different matter, and I've already told the Common Ground lady we'd be happy to have it there."

Betty Allsop disagreed: "We wanted it, and still want it, to be somewhere in the Dorset that Ken knew and loved. He never even saw Steep Holm."

Steep Holm tends to attract lost property. Generally it is items of clothing or lens caps; in one case the whole camera. The losers usually ring me as soon as they arrive home. Sometimes, however, the loss is not realised until much later.

"Hello Mr Legg," said the hesitant, soft male voice. "You don't know me, but I'm trying to find out some information about a trip you ran to Steep Holm in October."

"Which trip was it?" I asked.

"That's really why I'm ringing," he said. "It was in the middle of the week and there was a television crew with you. I need to know the precise date."

"What do you need to know that for?" I sensed something legal, fearing he was about to sue us for some calamity. October had been a troublesome month for weather but as far as I could recall all the trips had been carried out with the minimum of soakings and without other incidents. All the visitors had been returned to the mainland intact.

"It is embarrassing for me to tell you why," he went on, "but the only thing I need to know is the date of that trip."

Various memories came back to me of people on it, whom they had been talking to on the boat, and the general fun we all had on the island. It had been a good day. My thumb held the diary open on that Thursday: "Knightstone 8.00 to land near the top of an exceedingly high tide ... TV for day ... Sgt. John Shapley rang: he may take his son."

I could have given my caller the fact he required but I continued to press him for the reason. It seemed reasonable to ask why the date of that trip mattered so much.

"Well, it was the last time I saw my wife," he said. "We had married only a week and a half before. She met someone on that trip and never came home. I later had a phone call to say she had run away with someone she met on the boat. Now my solicitor is handling things and has asked me for a list of events and dates."

I gave him the date and apologised for being difficult. I did remember the girl, and where she had been sitting in the boat, but I puzzled over the identity of the male. None could be recalled as an obvious candidate and I had not noticed the magic of the body chemistry that was in the process of changing at least three lives. It hadn't even been a long day; we had left the island soon after noon. I have no information of how the new romance progressed, though I can tell you that neither of the pair has risked a return visit to Steep Holm.

Island stalwarts: Ken Cass (left) still worked on the island's plumbing at 80, with Bob Moon, the retired chief executive of Woodspring District Council, who also suffered hard-labour. The young lady giving him such an admiring glance is his wife, Pam. Photographed by Rodney Legg in 1991.

Hero: without unflappable boatman John Watts and his consummate mastery of one of the trickiest landing beaches in the British Isles we would long ago have faced disaster. His skills have plucked us from sweeping currents and storm-lashed rocks and carried us safely through the eye of the storm. Such exploits are taken for granted, or at least played down lest they frighten off the punters, such is his modesty and our ingratitude. Photographed, in *Silver Spray*, by Rodney Legg in 1991.

Strandings and hysteria

The closest that Steep Holm has come to being the lead item on News at Ten occurred on Monday 27 June 1983. It was the first of the big-ship visits to the island to go somewhat wrong. The paddle-steamer *Waverley* had disgorged an estimated seven hundred visitors and crew on to the island in the middle of the day. They had been ferried from the steamer, on to the island's beach, by the *Weston Lady* in loads of sixty at a time. Some were from Weston-super-Mare but the bulk were picked up in Penarth, which had been the *Waverley's* last port of call. The excessive interest was the combination of the romance of the newly refitted paddle-steamer and the mystery of an island so visible yet so remote from the Welsh coast. Few boats from South Wales had landed at Steep Holm since the Royal Artillery shuttle service of 1941-45. And this was a "nice" day.

The *Waverley*, however, was little more that day than an ultimate experience in queuing. There were queues that intersected other queues as everyone queued for something – coffee, snacks, the toilets and souvenirs – and the entire boat became an immobile throng of humanity. At Steep Holm they queued for out.

That exit, being ferried the last few hundred yards to shore by the *Weston Lady*, had been relatively painless and on Steep Holm they took the opportunity to throng together in the Barracks. Strangely there were sections of the island's paths that were completely empty as people collected elsewhere in amorphous biomass. They spent well on the island's stamps but there was a lack of the usual gift-shop range. "Where is the craft shop that we were told about on the boat?" one man asked. "I collect a commemorative tea-spoon from everywhere I visit!"

The disembarkation had started at about 2.30 pm and this first boat-load was due to return to the *Waverley* at 4.30 pm. It took an age as the wind picked up and the tide began to turn. The *Weston Lady* had to make numerous attempts at coming alongside the steamer and then break-off as the swell lifted her into the sides of the bigger boat's paddle-box.

I realised things were going slowly but the first indication I had of real problems was when a group of people I had seen on to the *Weston Lady* an hour-and-a-half before were coming up the path on to the top of the island.

"They couldn't get to the *Waverley*," the lady said. "Your boat was being thrown up and down by the waves. So he had to eventually give up and bring us back to the beach."

"Is it just you," I said. "Or are there some others as well?"
"God," she said, "there are hundreds! The beach is full of
people."

I went on to Tower and looked down. It was indeed like the
Dunkirk evacuation without the sand or any boats. Waves were
breaking across the beach, with spray blowing as the tips were
caught by the freshening wind. I then found a man on the rocks
who was wearing an ultra-large "PS *Waverley*" T-shirt with a
picture of the boat I could no longer see. He turned out to be a
stranded crewman. "Where is she?" I asked.

"*Waverley*'s gone to Penarth to pick-up an evening cruise," he
said, "and your boat's back at Weston to get some more beer."

The sun had gone from the beach and the dispirited mass was
beginning to realise that it had been abandoned. I ran to the
Barracks to unpack and unlock – it had been closed as we too
prepared for home – and the mob were in close pursuit. Panic
buying followed of everything – all the remaining drink, chocolates and "Pot Noodles". No one dared estimate the number of
people on the island; it ran into hundreds.

"I must get word to my school," a tall man said with all the
authority he could muster. "You must have an emergency telephone. There's a coach waiting for us."

All I could offer was a citizen band radio. Much to my sur-
prise his lads managed bring it to life (there had been some
problem with the aerial) and then to penetrate the inanities
("Cheroki Chief calling Serbonian Temptress for an eyeball").
Somehow, through the language of the primaeval bog, they
made contact with a thinking Neanderthal.

As for the other facilities, the toilets had blocked and the sum
total of island bedding was eighteen rather old mattresses, and
the warmth was from some hastily demolished elder bushes
that were being made to fit somewhat reluctantly into two small
grates.

What transpired would be told to the Weston Mercury by Mrs
Edna Murphy of Bleadon, who was far kinder to us than the
male callers who found my telephone number from the other
side of the Bristol Channel.

"I wondered if we were going to return at all," she said. "It
looked as though we would have to spend the night on the
island."

It was, as she remembered, dusk by the time the last load of
visitors had been plucked by the *Weston Lady* from the beach
and returned to the *Waverley*. By now the tide had almost
completed its cycle and most of the beach had been under water

for hours. There was little of it left, as Mrs Murphy would explain to the reporter: "We got off the island quite late in the evening – and by the time we did only a few feet of the beach could be seen. Everybody got off all right, but it was a close-run thing and a tricky operation to manage.

"The crews of both the *Weston Lady* and the *Waverley* were wonderful," the charitable Mrs Murphy continued. "The people from the Trust who run the island were also marvellous. It was quite a day!"

In the *Waverley* Captain David Neill gave the order to weigh anchor as the paddle turned and the black shape of a depopulated island was put behind us. There was a call to the paddle-steamer on the marine radio from Swansea Coast Guard. "Captain Neill," the voice said, "just to let you know there's press and television waiting when you get back to Weston." He thanked them for the warning. He would stay on the bridge at Weston and we slipped off amongst the last of the English contingent of visitors via the *Weston Lady* for the final hundred yards into Knightstone Causeway.

The Welsh parties would be home too late to hear what was only now the first item on the brief late-night local summaries. The nightmare turned into a celebration. It was the first time the Trust had banked a four-figure sum from a single day's efforts.

Subsequent strandings on the island have involved fewer people, though sometimes a disproportionate sense of panic. The "Emergency Shelter Fund" collection tin rattled around the homeward boat provided a total of £850 in the period 1982-89 and always did particularly well after those close-run exits where we had only just beaten the elements. It has bought fifty sleeping bags, to go with the bunks and mattresses purchased through the help of the Countryside Commission and Woodspring District Council, and there are also three cases of decent claret so that civilised values are maintained. Psychological needs are less easily serviced.

The withdrawal syndrome sets in as stays on Steep Holm that exceed twenty-four hours induce an irrepressible (there's a pun there) desire for media attention. One's suffering and eventual return – an event which recedes with every tide – have their counterpart on the mainland where grieving spouses brace themselves for News at Ten . . .

"CB Rescue" and "Island Rescue" the Star and The Sun reported on 25 April 1985. The Star's report was fractionally more informative than that of the competition: "Twelve wildlife enthusiasts, stranded for four days by storms on Steep Holm island in the Bristol Channel, were rescued yesterday after a CB fan picked up their SOS."

None of the reports bothered to spoil the story by saying that for three of those four days the party had been booked to stay on the island. In getting through the additional unscheduled night they had rummaged through our emergency stores and caused me to lose my last reminder of the summer of 1982.

Someone knew their wine. The casualty of that little episode was one superb bottle of claret, among the best of the acclaimed 1982 vintage, that had been given to me at Christmas by John Pitfield (who monitored the tabloids for the cuttings). It had a label saying it was not for sale, and was to be laid down for ten years – by which time it was hoped we might have an Inn reopening to celebrate. Perhaps it revived their spirits; c'est la vie.

Sometimes visitors do not stay on the island long enough to be stranded. "Noises in the night and ghost stories terrified two teenage girls alone on a deserted island in the Bristol Channel at the weekend," Peter de Ionno reported in the Western Daily Press on 22 June 1981. "Jane Williams and Vicky Phillips, both aged 16, had to be rescued by lifeboat during their first night on Steep Holm island bird sanctuary." It was hardly night, however, for 10 pm on Saturday 20 June 1981 was the middle of the summer and still light.

The girls sent up a distress flare. A passing yacht alerted the Coast Guards and Weston-super-Mare lifeboat was launched. John Watts found the girls stumbling down the cliff path to the South Landing and saying they were so frightened that they had been thinking of swimming home to Penarth.

What had caused them to flip? During the day the workers on the island had apparently told them of stories about the island's traditional ghost, the sixth-century hermit, St Gildas. They told me they had heard footsteps crunching the non-gravel surface of the path outside of the Barracks. There would certainly have been shrieking from the seabirds and quite possibly the barking of a Muntjac deer in the undergrowth at dusk. As they retreated indoors they had to come to terms with a huge, dark building that was without any electricity. The combination made for utter terror.

The girls insisted the island was haunted and Vicky Phillips would later detail her experience in the South Wales Echo of 26 September 1984 after the paper had asked its readers for their ghost stories:

"We set off for Steep Holm, excited but apprehensive. About

84

50 other visitors travelled across to the island but only for the day. During that day we discussed with the warden the conservation work that we could do. We were also shown the accommodation facilities and the safety equipment.

"At about 6 pm visitors left and we were alone. It was a funny feeling being left on the island, just two of us with a few thousand sea birds. However, we locked ourselves into the Barracks and settled down for the night.The only sounds to be heard were those of the seagulls and the tiny deer.

"We were just dropping off to sleep when a deathly silence occurred. For how long I cannot remember, but it was very eerie. It was then we heard the sound of shuffling footsteps – inside the Barracks – a sound which I shall never forget as long as I live. There was definitely "something" there – we were aware of a presence of some sort. We were both too scared to investigate, our first thought being to get outside straight away, although it was getting dark.

"There was no way we could go and stay inside again, so after much argument, we decided to summon help.The only means of communication was by a flare, the consequences of which were obvious, but it was either that or swim.

"The lifeboat from Weston-super-Mare wasted no time in getting us off the island, although being in such a hurry to get off I fell, ripping a large chunk out of my jeans and obtaining a large scar to my knee – a souvenir, no doubt! We didn't even stay long enough to sign the visitors' book!

"I shiver to think of those few hours we were alone on the island and believe me when you hear, see or experience anything like that it certainly can be a ghastly experience."

It led to questions about the wisdom of allowing young people to stay alone on the island. In this case the two girls had come with their parents, who departed with the day visitors, and pleaded to be allowed to stay for the weekend. I had to make my excuses to the Weston Mercury reporter: "The girls said they wanted to do conservation work. They had just finished their O-levels and seemed extremely rational and sensible. We have left males in twos on the island before and we have always tried to treat the sexes the same but it seems we'll have to think about this again."

The reporter had heard from someone else that we had also just had a problem with a solitary adult male. To quote the Weston Mercury of 26 June 1981: "The previous week a man a lot older had elected to stay on the island for seven days to follow his hobby of photography and ended by bitterly regretting his self-imposed isolation."

Vicky Phillips partly came to terms with her fear when she returned to Steep Holm for the day, after re-living that evening for the South Wales Echo. We made sure she was on the boat back at five o'clock, not that she wanted to stay for a repeat of the "ghastly experience".

The group of people most thankful to be rescued from the island were from the Bath Probation Service, doing a spell of community service, who had gone over on 9 March 1985. It became a long weekend and their anxiety was passed on to us by citizen-band radio enthusiast Paul Mason on the Somerset mainland. We would sail to retrieve them in the teeth of a north-westerly blowing at a chill factor below zero. As the seas abated somewhat we left at the promised time in an open boat. The wind was now carrying icy rain that was virtually sleet, almost horizontally and mixed with the equally cold spray.

John Watts steered the wheel with his back to it and the island, with just an occasional glance to the front, and we were, in the Dorset expression of my youth, "shrammed with the cold". We were soaked long before we left Weston Bay and that would take an age. The normal 40 minutes crossing-time was extending indefinitely as we came to a point two miles east of Steep Holm and about half a mile north-east from the South Patches buoy. At times we were not only failing to make head-way but were being pushed backwards. Lining up the Flat Holm lighthouse with its background landmarks on the Welsh mainland showed we had failed to make any progress in half an hour.

Eventually we did get to Steep Holm, but the crossing had taken three hours, and at the time they were looking for us we had remained such an insignificant speck that no one on the island had spotted us. They had carried all their gear back to the Barracks and were huddled in front of the fire.

When finally someone did see us splashing about offshore there was about ten minutes of frenetic activity. People with cases were scurrying up and down the cliff path. Finally there was no more downward movement between the trees and John Watts brought us into the beach. Waves were breaking over the boat as the lads and their leaders flung themselves towards us and into the sea.

We pulled them aboard like sacks of potatoes as their baggage came hurtling over our heads. I grabbed one of the leaders and pulled him over the side but he slithered face-first to the deck and I thrust my hand to cup his nose and glasses from the impact. Then it was over and we were riding the seas back into Weston.

"We were desperate," one of the boys told me. "I won't tell you what I've just offered to do for the last cigarette on the island!"

We were all almost dead from the wet and the cold when we landed. The compensation, however, was the subsequent revival of normal sensations. Strangely, it takes just twenty minutes into coffee and a radiator for the body to feel almost as if nothing as unbearable had ever happened. Nerves click-in as the system comes back on-line. It all seemed less real than a dream. The boys came by in Brian Lydford's mini-coach and the waves were this time of human relief.

Our ideal passage-boat for the island was the steel-plated *Ivanhoe*. She was formerly a ship's lifeboat, on the Shaw Saville liner *Ocean Monarch*, and had been provided with a small wheelhouse. Her practical advantage over our faithful wooden open-boat *Jane* was that she had sides that were raised above the usual splash-zone of the waters. Regulars began to shed their waders and oil-skins. For the latter part of the 1970s we had trips that were generally something not far removed from being dry.

Sometimes things nearly went wrong. Once, as a "Trip round the bay" found itself in an Atlantic depression, veteran boatman Frank Watts decided to evacuate the island; weather that had been forecast for France was blowing several hundred miles off-course and the situation was worsening. It was a skilful take-off into mounting waves but the bay trippers did not share our relief. Several were being sick, including one poor lady who had no more to bring up and was retching on the floor and screaming: "I wish I were dead!" Though the calm day had gone it was still deceptively sunny as we battled into Weston Bay.

That occasion was discomfort without danger. The latter came in 1980 when the boat was nearly shipwrecked on the island. She had come in to pick us up, as the wind veered and strengthened, coming from the north-east, and piled large waves sideways on to the beach. One caught the *Ivanhoe*'s stern and pushed her on to the beach as we were trying to climb aboard. The sea then crashed over her side. She was tossed broadsides on to the pebbles and I moved seawards of the bow with the painter – the mooring rope – in a pathetic attempt to pull her clear. I fell off in the undertow of a huge wave and was washed outwards.

The full predicament did not come home to me until years later when Mike Webber found a snapshot he had taken. It showed me floating like a bag of rags – which clinched the identification – behind the boat. Jenny Smith then told me that she had pulled me ashore. My only recollection is of the next stage, lying on the pebbles and watching in what seemed to be slow-motion as boatman John Watts heaved a rope through an eye-ring in semi-submerged rock as the waves broke around him.

Somehow they refloated the *Ivanhoe* but with dents and scrapes on the hull that would have proved terminal had she been constructed of the ubiquitous modern fibreglass. As for me, back in Weston I was mothered by the splendid Italian ladies of the Pescara Pizzeria, in St James's Street. I was compelled to shed my soaking rags. I was disappointed to have to return the borrowed clothes to their sons, a week later, and there has been no hope for my image ever since.

Another near miss was the time when an ordinary pick-up plunged us into mountainous seas which went well beyond all licence in what is euphemistically termed by the boatmen as "the South Patches roll". The *Ivanhoe* lurched sideways to the left and seemed overwhelmed as the sea came over the wheel-house and inside the ashtray, compass, matches and mugs were propelled horizontally. Waves continued to smash across us as the scale of the seas became magnified into crests and troughs that seemed house-sized. The dips were big enough to swallow all view of the mainland.

The wild sea ruled out any chance of disembarking at Anchor Head or waiting for water at Knightstone Causeway. As the only alternative we headed towards the semi-protected north side of Brean Down and peered through Dave Reid's Zeiss binoculars to try and make out the whisps of willow branches that mark the winding channel into the Axe estuary. Its grey walls of mud were visible for a few seconds and then inundated by the next great wave that broke across the half-mile of flats to Black Rock. The surging sea only relaxed its grip on the river as we reached the narrows at Uphill.

The severity of this full gale was even more apparent on land. First it was the blown sand and the effort required for hunched walking back into town. Then, beside Weston's Beach Lawns, the metal panels of the bus-shelters burst off their rivets and skidded at knee-level across the road. It was an awesome demonstration of the power of the wind.

The autumn gales, on 19 September 1981, would claim the *Ivanhoe*. She had on that occasion brilliantly executed a perfectly timed pick-up that had lifted us off the island and brought us to the lee shore of the old pier at Birnbeck Island before the full fury of the weather had erupted. As she was anchored, for what would be the last time, the size of the seas was visibly swelling. Late that evening the combination of tide and wind piled such a volume of water under the boat that she snapped her mooring rope. Next morning she was found wedged in the rocks up-Channel, on Sand Point, and made her final television appearance. The hull that had withstood the battering of beach pebbles was fatally twisted and peppered with fractures. She would be floated home but only for scrap.

Her successor, *Weston Lady*, was similar in shape but had a fibreglass hull. That the 1980s treated her so tenderly was partially due to John Watts's seamanship and equally because of the greatly improved accuracy of the coast weather warnings. Satellite pictures and their computer interpretations have – the odd 1987 hurricane excepted – brought a precision to the forecasts that compels respect and observance.

Sometimes the uncomfortable memories of a Steep Holm visit surface on the mainland. In 1984, Woodspring Council's Leisure and Tourism director Clive Jackson told his committee that they were invited, once again, to "risk a fact-finding trip" to the island. Councillor Mrs Mary McEwan-Smith recalled the "terrible crossing" of the previous occasion.

"I got soaking wet on the journey," she said. "The boatman said they had never lost a passenger and I said there was always a first time. You have a job to get on the island because of the beach, and the Barracks are terrible." Then, showing a charitable lack of malice, she added: "I think we should spend money on it!" The councillors voted a £1,000 grant, since renewed and increased, towards the renovation work and the rebuilding of the Inn as a beach store for first-aid and emergency equipment.

One of the island's near misses for Channel shipping was in the mid-1980s when a captain ignored his Admiralty chart and cut across the shingle spit at the east end of the island. It was towards high water and she would have passed about 150 feet from the shore but there was insufficient depth for the manoeuvre. She must have been a largish vessel, that had somehow come up the Bristol Channel and gone right instead of left of our obstacle, or a coaster out of Bridgwater that had cut the corner between the South Patches buoy and the island but come too close to the latter.

Whatever the cause of the miscalculation she had hit the shingle at a right-angle and the impact had gouged a trench three feet deep that ran across the spine of the central part of the gooseneck. Some exceedingly large boulders, weighing several hundredweight, had been pushed sideways.

That was nearly a prize catch for us. Frequently the lesser yachtsmen ignore these turbulent waters at their peril. There is a widespread inability among the fraternity to perceive that when in a calm sea you come across a patch of choppy water it is there because some obstacle is disrupting the tidal momentum – id est, it is shallow. Normally it costs them no more than time, waiting to refloat if they do it on a dropping tide, but it punctured the bottom of George Caney's motor boat from Penarth and had us transferring his passengers at sea. Other times the yachtsmen ignore the rise and force of the turning tide and lose an anchor or even their craft.

An unmanned yacht floated upstream from the island but fortuitously for two despairing Welshmen, screaming from the island's beach, our own boat happened to be approaching. She picked us up and then pushed upstream in pursuit. It was only as the yacht was about to run aground off Sand Point that we were able to grab her. We were all thoroughly soaked in the process and it had been tricky as well as uncomfortable.

The boatmen asked £7 for their trouble but yachtsmen take the precaution of never carrying cash. Experiences, however, are never wasted, and apart from advising the boatmen to take an Open University course in the law of marine salvage, I now actively discourage any heroics in the cause of saving property. In 1987 we watched helplessly from the Inn as a rotund gentleman nearly drowned in the tide-race whilst failing to retrieve a beach-ball.

I know the drone of an approaching Westland Wessex helicopter to foretell disaster. Occasionally, however, it is a red one of the Royal flight en route home to one of the mansions in Gloucestershire. The yellow ones are more common and these are about the last of the Wessex aircraft in military service. Their rôle is air-sea rescue. One provided the lesson about not underestimating those waters when she spent the morning checking out the wreckage of the *Amanda Kay* which was floating past the island. It was the aftermath of a bank holiday weekend gale which, I think, had also claimed Edward Heath's *Morning Cloud*. Our lost yacht had broken up between Flat Holm and Steep Holm, possibly after hitting a rock or floating wood, but strong seas can also feel like a solid obstacle.

The search was for three or four bodies and it went on for several days until they became bloated with decomposition and were washed ashore. The only survivor made his landfall at

Hinkley Point. That time we talked to the helicopter via radio telephone, which was the only emergency during which the linkage worked, but in 1987 I was appointed an Auxiliary Coast Guard for the purpose of communicating with their Swansea command on the service's internal Channel-O marine band.

Spectacular exits are passé. It is much more unusual for anyone to arrive in style. Sometimes I have had to leap into a cleft in the rocks at South Landing and alternately pull the boat in as a wave ebbs and then push her seawards as the next wave comes in. That, however, is hardly a dignified entrance for the visitors as they are helped over the bows and then have to scale the rocks. Ordinarily, the beach landing is uneventful with a simple walking of the plank down on to the pebbles, though even that can have some young males trembling.

The best ever entrance to the island in modern times was "Operation Sweetholm" in 1976 which was arranged for me by Major Jim Bilton of 25 Field Battery of 19 Field Regiment, Royal Artillery, based at Larkhill on Salisbury Plain. He had just run the endless permutations of the computer programme to see if Nato's central front was still defensible and turned his attention to invading Steep Holm for the day. I don't think I had told anyone, certainly not our chairman who stood at the bow with his binoculars scanning for Wild Leek flower-heads and the outreach of a Peregrine from the rocks to protest our arrival.

Major Bilton's men were behind us, converging on our boat from both sides in high-speed inflatables. They zoomed in front of our bows as we came into the beach. "What on earth's going on?" John Fowles asked. "Just a little welcome for you," I said.

At that moment there was a military backdrop. Two Lockheed Hercules transport planes of the Royal Air Force came from the north-east at height over the island.

"Watch the first plane," I told John. "The parachutists should drop any second."

"Oh God, what have you done?" he responded.

The remark about the paratroops was only my little joke, the arrival of the Hercules aircraft being purely coincidental, but John Fowles remained tense for the rest of the day. As we walked on to the top of the island, at Tombstone Battery, a wiry young man with camouflaged face and combat jacket appeared in front of us from the bushes. "Good morning, sir," he addressed Major Bilton. "I thought I would come the direct route up the cliffs!"

About the only subsequent entrance to the island to upstage the day of the Army games came in 1987 when Rose Sparrow, from Uphill, literally leapt into our lives. She became the auxiliary tea-lady, a highly important island post, on that first day. Initially, however, we wondered what had descended upon us. Rose, it transpired, had missed the boat. Not being short on initiative she then persuaded the boatmen to take her out to Steep Holm on a later bay-trip that was not scheduled to land.

In fact, when they arrived at the island there was such a strong force of tide running across the beach that it was impossible for the boat to come in – we saw from the Inn that they had given up an approach attempt and were backing off.

On the bows, however, there was a woman and she was struggling with the older boatman, John (Kenny) Watts, as his son, John Watts junior, reversed the boat out of difficulty. "You can't do that!" Kenny shouted.

She did! The female dropped off the bow with billowing skirts, bolt upright and straight into the water as the boat continued to edge away from the beach. The figure then flung herself into the waves and splashed the final 40 feet to the beach. The Sparrow had landed.

Shuttle-service: paddle-steamer *Waverley* offshore and *Silver Spray* running into the surf on the island beach to pick-up visitors for return to the larger vessel. Seen from the north, from the former beer-garden of the Inn (right) with Tower Rock rising in the background. Photographed by Rodney Legg in 1991.

Blowing up the island

Onshore, the days of greatest excitement have been when the island has rocked to explosions. These have sometimes been a daily and even an hourly event as in 1980-87 an immense quantity of commercial gelignite and the mouldable plastic-type military Demex produced on the Somerset side of the water by the Royal Ordnance Factory at Puriton have crunched their way through rocks and girders. The reason has always been a compelling matter of public safety, as with an overhang of the cliff that was collapsing on to the steps up from the beach, and the lattices of steelwork that were intended to protect the wartime Royal Artillery gunners from German fighter-bombers were disintegrating around parties of visitors.

Curiosity brought people inside these structures, as did the need to shelter from the rain, and sometimes a whole group would clamber on to a precarious roof to enjoy the view. That they had to go became apparent when, on one of the visits from the Countryside Commission – who were considering paying towards the cost of the clearance operation – a girder conveniently decided to crash to ground and shatter into a cloud of rust. That piece of perfect timing also had a VIP onlooker and was witnessed by Sir Derek Barber, the chairman of the Commission.

Because they were by now considered to be buildings of historical or architectural interest we had to apply for listed building consent. Bob Moon, the chief executive of Woodspring District Council, was sympathetic and in no mood to serve us with a "repairs notice" to bring them back into reasonable condition. Neither was the Environment Department, whose architect was more wary of them than any other visitor we have had on the island.

I had offered to go underneath one of the canopies and pick off handfuls of rust from the steel beams. "I do not need to go inside to see that they are dangerous," he said curtly.

His off-the-cuff estimate for their removal and replacement – "as a replica, because they are impossible to repair" – was £250,000 apiece; a cool million for what most visitors, rightly, regarded as an eyesore. Our duty to history would be assuaged by the use of the camera, with Colin Graham spending a week on the island to photograph them from every conceivable angle apart from that for which they were designed – the sky – for the National Monuments Record.

One time in blowing up the island we nearly detonated ourselves. It was the occasion of removing the 1941-built pier supports from the middle section of the beach. These had been denuded of pebbles by storms and the concrete protruded a couple of feet above the general beach level. At the corner there was the projecting tip of an 'H'-shaped steel girder and bent pipe stuck up behind. This was a serious obstacle to landings and departures on the beach, particularly on days when the sea was liable to drag the boat sideways; and at other times it was an unseen hazard that the boatmen had to try to keep in mind.

The Amey Roadstone Corporation quarrymen, led by Mike Webber, excavated a cavity under the offending lump of concrete. They were using only a few pounds of explosive and on past experience of the island bangs it was expected to be a relatively small explosion. Nonetheless we went through the full safety procedures. I blocked off the steps down to the eastern side of the island and told the archaeologists at the Priory that we would soon be ready. They asked to carry on working, given that the previous explosions had been so localised and the top of the island had not been previously touched by any far-flung debris. Nearer the scene we disturbed the gulls from their eggs. One of the quarrymen was going to take a picture of the explosion from the quay wall but decided against it. "There is just a chance of a splinter of rock ricochetting off the cliff," Mike Webber said. "That will go into you like a bullet!".

All of us, and the detonator, squeezed inside the little 1941-built telephone exchange, which had the protection of an opening towards the cliff-face rather than the sea, and had been "hardened' to withstand aircraft cannon-fire. On the other hand those advantages were somewhat discounted by the fact that the foundations had collapsed on the seaward side into the old Inn and there was an overhang of two to three feet that was now suspended in space. Chris Maslen and Jenny Smith were crammed with me into the back of the tiny room.

The bang that followed was the loudest I have ever heard. Its pressure waves punched our ears and left them deafened and ringing. The island shook and it felt as if the telephone exchange was tipping backwards into the void beneath. Then it rained pebbles and fragments of rock. The ground outside the telephone exchange was until that moment the clearest piece of path on the entire island, because I had picked up even the smallest stones for some walling beside it, but it was now covered with pieces of freshly-fractured rock.

Andrew Buncombe came down from the Priory to report that stones had fallen out of the sky all around them. In fact he was

94

still reminding me of the fact years later. By then, with immediate application, we had an effective blasting procedure – that all those not involved were accounted for in the Barracks and kept inside that building until operations were over. For that afternoon, however, we all had our near misses to recount. The boatmen would bring stories of the noise and vibration which shook windows six miles away in Weston-super-Mare. That I admit to this in print is with the benefit of knowing that the six years of chapter 16 of the Statute of Limitations, 1623, and its successor legislation now preclude any actions. Our insurers subsequently re-drafted their cover to specifically exclude those days on which we have explosions on the island.

Upon realising we were alive, and hearing the protests of the gulls, we staggered down to the beach. I then realised the initiative that an attacker has in a war and that a soldier in such a situation would then have to brace himself to fight. Whatever it had done to our adrenalin, the outcome was that we were only fit for laughing. I didn't take Andrew seriously but on reflection I should have hugged him – a potential tragedy had been relegated to an experience. There were boulders on the quay wall where the quarryman had intended standing to take his photographs.

Below was a huge crater. Mike Webber, himself a bulky hulk, posed in it for pictures. It was a cup-shaped hole about 25 feet wide and 15 feet deep. Disappointingly, it would be filled by the tide by the time the boat came back for us, and by the next visit the sea had largely filled it with pebbles and reduced it to just a depression. For the moment, however, we had a hole and its post-mortem to consider. The steel pipe, of which only a couple of feet had been showing, turned out to be 14 feet long. Mike had thought his explosive had been packed into loose pebbles but in fact he had stuffed it into a chamber beneath the concrete. This had then contained the explosion; the weakest point for the force to take was under and outwards from the point of blast. We made use of the hole by rolling some rocks into it. These lesser obstructions to our boating would come back to the surface in 1988 after the beach profile had changed with the central section being scoured and its pebbles heaped at the high-tide mark. Such things are cyclical.

Mike Webber's men were to have a different pattern of experiences on 9 March 1985. The verses that follow commemorate the delights of boating in the Bristol Channel as experienced by the Amey Roadstone Corporation's shot-blasters who arrived on the island a little later than intended. The quarrymen then found that the flak-tops to the 1941 gun batteries were rather stronger than anyone had thought. Len Poole put their thoughts to paper:

It was Saturday the ninth I know,
I can remember it quite well.
The tide it was just rolling in,
There was hardly any swell.

So Mike set off from Batts Combe,
Together with his crew,
To blow up some old buildings
That the Germans could not do.

They loaded up the frail old boat,
Which was of course on loan,
And singing "Old Sea Shanties",
Set off to find Steep Holm.

Now this old boat she tossed and turned,
And nearly went aground,
But after only one mile out,
The motor it broke down.

The fog it grew so quickly,
As they drifted helplessly.
But Len said "Now come on lads,
Let's sing 'Abide with me'."

They all sat there so mournfully,
And all were afraid to speak,
Until Len said, "Oh, bother me,
The boat has sprung a leak!"

They bailed and pumped out furiously,
And Len took up the stroke,
But what he didn't know was that
The bilge pump it was broke.

They drifted on for quite some time,
Until Michael said, "That's queer,
We started off from Weston,
And we're now at Clevedon Pier!"

The tide turned in their favour,
And they set off with a roar,
A mere five and a half hours later,
They landed on Steep Holm shore.

Our heroes were undaunted,
As they laid their charges down,
And the following explosion
Blew a daisy to the ground.

Now all they have left for the lubbers,
And their efforts were quite a bit,
Was an earwig with a broken leg,
And a pile of seagull shit!

Not all trips to the island go quite that well. Quite often we never arrive at all. Nor, it should be added, does this testimony apply to our regular boatmen – they were piloting another craft at the time. And also went via Clevedon.

On the only occasion when we had wanted a bang to be noticed by the mainland it turned out to be a whimper. Chris Maslen had got into difficulties trying to reach his converted Royal Navy landing craft, a former test-torpedo recovery vessel, which was moored off the South Landing. We heard that he was in a dinghy off the beach and struggling without oars to extricate himself from the tide-race. I grabbed a distress flare and ran with Jenny Smith to the top of Tower Rock from where we saw his predicament. He was baling out water and not far short of sinking.

I fired the flare. It went off with a loud enough report but I did not realise it had failed to explode properly with a red flash in the sky. By a remarkable coincidence, John Pitfield, who had delivered these life-saving fireworks from the makers, Pains-Wessex, happened to be on the island. "That didn't work," he told me, but I failed to grasp his meaning. Instead of running for another flare I stood there like a dummy watching Chris prepare to swim. He was then able, however, to empty out the tiny craft as the tide began to slacken.

"Oh, so you were the cause of that noise!" Joan Rendell said as she saw the spent flare-case in my hand. Jenny Smith did not seem to realise, either, that despite the bang the thing had not performed correctly in the sky. "Anyway," she said as laconically as usual, "by the time anyone gets here it's going to be all over." Chris gradually managed to paddle back to the island, with his hands, and recovered on the beach.

He would later put Jenny to within an inch of her life, literally, with an 80 pound boulder. Chris heaved it on to a wall at the Inn for me, but it slipped forward, and at the same moment Jenny walked under the other side of the wall. She looked up at me, and opened her mouth to ask something: "Do you ... " "Stand still!" I screamed as it fell fractionally in front of her head – she felt the slipstream – and the stone impacted beside her feet. The bulging top of the wall had helped project the stone further forwards – had my building observed normal vertical and horizontal conventions Jenny would have become our first fatality.

It is ourselves that we find on an island. For me the disconcerting reality had been the extent of the changeability. In the early 1980s I relished the loneliness, being utterly at personal peace when alone on the island, poised on the top of a cliff wall, directly above the waves, and finishing my last bucket of cement in the dark, at 11.15 pm as the *Waverley* paddle-steamer – lit like a Christmas tree – clipped the corner of the island on her return to Penarth. By the mid-1980s it was the reverse feeling that prevailed. I have then missed the special person in my life.

Isolation is like alcohol in that it does not induce moods so much as accentuate the feelings one already has. Apart from thinking about that absent person, or cat, I have never missed television, radio, newpapers, electric light, telephone, typewriter or food. In my rather limited experience it has turned out to be the first place on earth where the vacuum cleaner has been successfully disinvented. That, in itself, may not be an answer to everything in life, but it is something.

It would be misleading, however, to imply that this offshore island is at peace from man's environment. The Royal Air Force flies weekdays and a section of Tornados – two warplanes, that is – beats up the island two or three times almost every day. The art of watching them is to look far to the side of the sound which comes from their historic position. The breathtaking treat to turn any boy's stomach is when a pair on the homeward run, back up the Bristol Channel, split and pass one to the south and one to the north side of the island at 50 feet above the sea. Seen from the Inn they then come out of the cliffs on both sides, within a second of each other, and ahead of their sound. By the time that reaches us they have crossed over, right over left, and are streaking towards the Severn Bridge at 700 miles per hour

The lumbering giants are the four-engined turbo-prop Lockheed Hercules transport planes, of which sixty are based at Lyneham in north Wiltshire, and their passage beside the island is sometimes half-way down the southern cliffs. Then, from the Barracks, you can start to count the rivets.

The Steep Holm year of the Hercules was from April onwards in 1982 when they maintained the shuttle service to Ascension

Island and the South Atlantic's winter war. All the aircraft had flight refuelling pods. They would for a few months make the previously unknown Ascension, just over the Equator, into the world's busiest airport. Steep Holm was their last piece of England at the beginning of the 4,000 miles to Wideawake (American) air station on British-owned Ascension and then the final 4,000 miles into the war zone. Chris Maslen and Jenny Smith were on the island throughout the time it was an emergency air route, as they repaired and redecorated the Barracks.

The Empire strikes back! Our minor contribution to the sideshow at this end was my permission to the Royal Navy Air Station at Yeovilton that they could exercise their Sea Kings at Steep Holm in island-assault practice runs. I don't know whether they ever did much around the island, though one pilot came low and waved when I was working at the top of the wall at the Inn, and in the midsummer of 1982 there hardly seemed to be a helicopter left in England.

As for the disturbance of the wildlife, aircraft noise and explosions are much less disconcerting than the general ambling presence of human beings – as is proved by the rare-breed species count on many of the country's gunnery ranges – and the Steep Holm experience is that the best successes of the Peregrines and other special birds have coincided with sustained bouts of blasting. No one else, however, is convinced.

At the times when we are having interminable explosions on the island I have to fend off the inevitable semi-hostile observation: "It must upset the birds!" Then I not only point out that they are used to the military sound effects but mention the much less localised effects of a decent thunderstorm. These are never more dramatic than when one is at sea in a little boat with forks of lightning descending to water all around you. We had one crossing when our evening return coincided with sustained lightning more or less directly overhead for the whole five miles.

"I think people should be told not to sit under the mast," Ken Cass said, "in case it gets hit."

"There's not much point in moving them," boatman John Watts answered. "If the mast is hit then we are all dead."

In another electrical storm, right over the island in the middle of the day on 14 May 1983, all our hair stood literally on end. People started noticing things were happening to others' heads without realising it was also occurring on their own. The most splendid example of the phenomenon was Jenny Smith whose black strands lifted ten inches skywards. We stood outside the

Barracks admiring each other and were told by Colin Graham and Ken Cass how stupid we were being. In the event the wrath of the gods did not zap our mini-ionosphere.

Electrical phenomenon: this was happening to the hair of all of us as we stood outside the Barracks, though longer (up to a foot, straight up) in the case of Jenny Smith. She is normally photogenic and does not remotely resemble a witch. Photographed by Colin Graham in May 1983.

We print stamps!

It is doubly fortuitous that the Post Office shows no inclination to deliver mail to Steep Holm. Firstly it is pleasant because for me, being an author for most of the week is nothing more than the most menial form of office work imaginable, and I do not go to Steep Holm in order to spend the day answering correspondence. Secondly, it opens for us the benefits of a loophole in the Post Office's legal monopoly.

They have authorised, or rather they have no legal power to prevent, the island issue of its own stamps and postmarks for the transit of mail to the mainland. The Post Office is reluctant to admit that these little perforated pieces of sticky paper are "stamps" at all – they always use the term "local carriage labels". To us, and the Oxford English Dictionary, they are postage stamps.

Where the confusion arises for visitors is that the Steep Holm stamps are only paying for the transport of the item of mail for the six miles from the post-box in the island Barracks to an official Post Office mail box on the seafront at Weston-super-Mare. For that journey we issue a stamp and cancel it with our own dated postmark – "STEEP HOLM, BRISTOL CHANNEL". If there is a problem with collection then we have an explanatory cachet, "Delayed by storm".

Onwards from Weston, however, it requires an official mainland stamp – one with the Queen's head, to the correct current rates – for the remainder of its passage which will be through the normal Post Office system. That applies, to the bafflement of some visitors, even if the address is on the promenade at Weston. It would be unlawful for us to deliver letters on the mainland. Fortunately, if the regulations are ever relaxed, it will remain impracticable.

Though the Post Office donated the George VI post-box which was placed in the Barracks they insisted that it was painted in colours other than the usual red, in order to lessen the official connection. Similarly the pre-partition post-boxes in the Irish Republic are now green. Jenny Smith painted ours much more elegantly, in black with gold relief, but the situation still confuses many visitors. Sometimes they fail to double-stamp the items and, if we have the time, we stick on the missing mainland or island stamp. Other times, when we are busy, the mail has to take its chances.

The Post Office asks that on postcards the island stamp is put on the "correspondence corner" of the card so that their stamp is alone in its usual place. That is because they are sensitive to the philatelic implications of their franking our stamp. Similarly they would take a dim view of our postmark touching the Queen's stamp, so distancing the two stamps helps with the practicalities of postmarking the mail.

Collectors frequently ask for details of the island stamp issues and frankings. That side of the business has been handled for the Trust by Nigel Keegan of Yeovil. Unlike some doubtful, and a few completely spurious, operations which have seized upon remote Scottish islands, we have chosen Lundy as our rôle model. It pioneered the private stamp in the 1930s though, unlike us, it adopted "puffin" as the euphemism for "penny". What Lundy has is credibility because the bulk of its carriage is genuine, on normal mail from the island, rather than contrived for the philatelists. Likewise Steep Holm has now put many thousands of items – more than a thousand at a time on some of the *Waverley* paddle-steamer days – through the national postal service.

Steep Holm stamps are from Steep Holm, though we get consequential bleatings from the purists about marks and crumpling in the course of progress through the system. Nigel Keegan pressed us to produce the first issue, though long before that time Bournemouth solicitor Ian McQueen had been suggesting the idea. Both were right that it would make both publicity and money though the returns have levelled off in recent years as the over-production of stamps which have come from offices a whole county away from the islands that ostensibly issued them have destroyed collector confidence. That is why our initial burst of issues has not been followed by others that were in the pipeline. It is disappointing because none of the island's obvious subjects – the Wild Peony, Peregrine and Herring Gull – have yet made it on to a stamp.

The first set of "STEEP HOLM" stamps was issued on 27 September 1980. They comprised a print of "Beach and Inn 1850" on the 12p; "Kenneth Allsop, 1971' photographed by Colin Graham on the 18p; "Zebra camouflage, 1943" showing the Rudder Rock searchlight post on the 30p; and "Packet boat *Ivanhoe*,1980", photographed by Stan Rendell, on the 40p. A sepia-tone first day cover was produced that features an enlarged version of the 12p print with a space blanked out from the sea for the address. Down the side it has details of the island: "Formerly owned by the Hon Mrs Ziki Robertson, heiress to the estate of the late Lord and Lady Wharton, it was given for ecological research in memory of the naturalist and broadcaster Kenneth Allsop. John Fowles, author of *The French Lieutenant's Woman*, is chairman of the Kenneth Allsop Memorial Trust. Vice chairman is Betty Allsop." Ziki Robertson, John Fowles and Betty Allsop each signed fifty of these covers. The cancellations are a round franking on some and a square "STEEP HOLM, BRISTOL CHANNEL" on others.

The first-day cover was reissued a year later with two over-stampings. The larger reads "1st ANNIVERSARY OF POSTAL SERVICE. STEEP HOLM 27-9-81" and the second is a sad postscript across the stamp that shows our former ferry, "IVANHOE SHIPWRECKED 19th Sept 1981".

Nigel Keegan also issued a hundred postcard versions. The colourful picture-map is of "The Weston Coast" and the island's 18p, 30p and 40p stamps appear on the back, along with the island's square franking, the anniversary stamping, and the Ivanhoe cancellation. These went through the national mails as well and carry a highly appropriate Queen's stamp, featuring an offshore fishing boat.

Another one hundred postcards featuring "The Weston Coast" were issued with a 15½p national commemorative stamp of "Henry VIII/Mary Rose" and put through the island and Post Office mails on 27 September 1982. They have a new, bolder, round franking and "2nd ANNIVERSARY OF POSTAL SERVICE. STEEP HOLM 27-9-82". Three island stamps were used, the 18p, 30p and 40p. The latter being inappropriate after the shipwreck it carries the stamping "New Mailboat MV Weston Lady EASTER 1982".

Meanwhile, more island stamps have been issued. The first-day cover for "Butterflies of Steep Holm" gave their story: "Gordon Beningfield, the artist for the official Post Office issue of butterfly stamps, has also painted the set for Steep Holm in the Bristol Channel. They are a celebration of our wildlife and a warning that many species are being endangered by widespread clearance of habitats and indiscriminate use of farm chemicals. These stamps are issued as the Wildlife and Countryside Bill is passing through Parliament. In many ways it offers too little, and comes too late."

Each of the island's four stamps carries Gordon Beningfield's name (unlike those of the Post Office) and our selection of species was the Red Admiral for the 14p, Tortoiseshell at 20p, Peacock at 30p, and Painted Lady at 44p. There had been a miscalculation during the design process; the amounts should have added up to £1. Our version of the Peacock turned out in stronger colours than that for the Post Office, and to strengthen the island connection I had sent Gordon some Henbane leaves. A somewhat spongy package broke over the mat when Betty Beningfield retrieved the post. I had also enclosed a Steep Holm pebble but that did not go into the finished designs.

Gordon donated the proceeds from sale of the originals – except that for the Peacock which he sent me with strict instructions that it was a personal gift, for my wall. He also refused to accept any fee for the stamps and compounded the donation by providing a further painting that was sold for the Trust's funds. There was also a secondary Allsop connection as Gordon Beningfield's encouragement and gifts were largely responsible in buying Powerstock Common, which Kenneth Allsop had saved from clear-felling, as a nature reserve. Gordon would be even more of an asset if we can ever helicopter him to the island – he would have to be brought that way as he has a terror of sailing.

Five hundred special first day covers were issued with all eight of Gordon's butterfly stamps, those from the Post Office (14p, 18p, 22p and 25p) as well as the island set. These are utterly authentic as they carry, in addition to the square Steep Holm franking, the official Post Office cancellation, "FIRST DAY OF ISSUE 13 MAY 1981 BRISTOL".

The next set featured the island's mammals. On the 14p is the Hedgehog – a very friendly little girl who was photographed by Stan Rendell as she clambered over a rock at the Priory. He also took two other photographs. The 18p has a Rabbit, also on Steep Holm. "Muntjac deer" at 28p are three-dimensional enough, and browsing on island elders, but happen to be stuffed. I bought them at Christie's and they came to Steep Holm via my next-door neighbour's garden. "Be quiet, Julie," I had whispered to her when she spotted them in the cabbages, "or they'll run away!" Only the "Grey seal" at 40p had no genuine island connection, being a picture bought from a wildlife photographic agency, though there were seals in the browner waters off Steep Holm when we issued an unperforated proof-version of the stamps on 5 September 1981. This was followed by the proper issue on 12 September and both carry the square postmark on a sepia tone first day cover that features the Hedgehog. Those of the proof-issue that went through the national mails have the stamping "WESTON-SUPER-MARE 11.15 PM 6 SEPT 1981 AVON.A" with "COLLECT BRITISH STAMPS – WORLD'S GREATEST HOBBY" overprinting the faces of the Prince and Princess of Wales on their 14p "29 July 1981" wedding day issue.

The fourth issue of Steep Holm stamps, also a series of four, had Susan Guy's paintings. These are primitive in style and show a variety of ships passing the island. A ''Viking longship'' is the 15p value, ''SS *Great Britain*'' at 18p, ''PS *Glen Avon*'' at 25p (but wrongly showing the paddle-steamer with two funnels; a dozen people wrote to point out she only had one), and HMS *Steepholm''* at 40p.

They were released on 22 February 1982 with a first day cover showing ''DV17'' – His Majesty's Trawler *Steepholm*,1943-60 – setting out from an East Coast port, Sheerness in all probability, to clear wrecks. The panel of words, on the theme of ''Maritime Bristol'', ends with a mention of the island and John Fowles: ''The chairman of its management trust is better known, on both sides of the Atlantic, as the author of the acclaimed novel and film *The French Lieutenant's Woman* – author John Fowles.'' He signed a few of these covers.

That, to date, is the postal history of Steep Holm in recent times. It was not quite in the league of commercial television, as ''a licence to print money'', but for a small offshore nature reserve it has done just that. In the process the stamps have been a novelty and a souvenir for thousands of island visitors and their friends.

Printing money: at least that was the idea, before the bubble burst. Most of the stack is blank paper – to make the picture look impressive – rather than stamps. Printers Brian Nicolson (left) and Stephen Taylor (right) of Surdaw Press, Gillingham, Dorset, with Rodney Legg in the middle. Photographed by Colin Graham in April 1980.

People problems

These books about the island have been compiled as we approach the twentieth anniversary of Ken Allsop's death. Inevitably we are now judged by our record.

We have, on Steep Holm, saved the island's endangered rarities so that they have a place in the twenty-first century, and we have made its history presentable. The intention is that it should be a continuing memorial; managed according to Ken's priorities which put wildlife first and people second.

The tales I have recounted, sometimes against ourselves, show that we have encouraged both day-trippers and long-stay visitors. The feedback has usually been rewarding. I recorded the instance of the island's precipitating a divorce but there was also a letter I forwarded to John Fowles, then our chairman, telling of how it had brought about a marriage. Other couples have made nostalgic returns and mentioned on the boat that they met on the island. Indeed I lost my companion from Wincanton, Karen Eden, to Richard Wike from Bristol. The irony was that they were both reluctant visitors, Karen having wanted to spend the day shopping in Weston, and Richard, who worked with Chris Maslen, was finally responding to endless invitations.

The Steep Holm community of the week beginning 26 August 1978 comprised Prebendary Ian Calvert and Reverend Horace Harper from Staffordshire, with Reverend Nomleas Sekonga of the Solomon Islands and a flock of thirteen. They printed their experiences in *Steep Holm – the record of a community holiday*.

They were marooned with eight gramophone records of punk-rock. The Augustinian canons set the pace, with holy communion at 05.30: "After a lapse of seven centuries, the praises of God in the liturgy of the English church rose again from Steep Holm, morning and evening. We worked on our domestic chores, and improved the island's paths and buildings. When tidal currents allowed, we went swimming, and held on the feast of St Giles, the patron saint of cripples, a handicap run round the island." The swimming was against the rules, but they became island-wise: "The currents around the island are swift, and from the vantage-point above the sea which the island provides, we thought we could detect boundaries within the water and minor whirlpools. It was safe to swim, provided we did not venture too far out, and avoided the hour before and after high-tide."

Sea-washed sugar provided a continuing reminder of the

crossing. Cooking by candlelight was not without its problems and the pattern of the days gradually adjusted to make full use of the natural light. Their most precarious path was 208 Steps where they shovelled loose rocks into the sea. The messiest objective was the removal of what was euphemistically termed a compost heap, "and, hopefully, its colony of flies". The Polynesian islander led the entertainments: "After supper, Nomleas Sekonga introduced us to dancing in his style: we did not quite feel up to introducing him to ours."

They floated a wooden cross on the waters as they waited for "the speck on the horizon which would grow into a boat". They felt they had shared the heartbeat of the island and that they were returning from "a holiday to lie snugly in the memory, and one in which, most of us acknowledge, the finger of God had touched us".

Other groups have combined the island experience with science. Michael Wagner brought a dozen sixth-formers from Rodway School, Mangotsfield, on 6 July 1981 and they carried out a photographic survey of the colour variation in the gulls' eggs, a lichen study of the walls of the ruins, a woodlouse marking project, and an experiment in marking and displacing the limpets to test their homing abilities. A secondary aggravation for the unfortunate limpets was a "shell-angle investigation to test the theory that it alters with exposure to wave action". They seem to have stopped short of eating them.

My greatest pleasure was sharing the excitement of the black boys from London who came to stay on the island on 12 July 1981. Boat journeys have shaped the history for the blacks of the British Empire but for these lads it was their first and an escape from the capital's current turmoil. One called himself "Desmond Dread" and gave his address as "Riot Area, Brockley". He commented: "Good away from riots. Bad beds, bad boat crossing. Too many seagulls. No mashed up shops and no reggae bands."

Many experienced island-hoppers have come to Steep Holm and remarked upon our relaxed atmosphere. David Church, from Banbury, contrasted it in 1982 with a staying visit on an island where he had to leap on to the rocks at the end of a sickening boat journey. The warden's wife was there to greet them: "These are the rules!"

He later received disapproving looks when he failed to give a positive answer to the question: "What will be your speciality for study during the week?"

A member of the party produced a cricket bat and was told:

"This is a nature reserve, not a recreation ground."

This reception led to a unifying of the visitors against the wardens, though as on Steep Holm, by the middle of the week, both temporary and permanent residents shared a common wish not to mix with day visitors to the island, whom they regarded as intruders, keeping themselves at a distance of several hundred yards from the trippers.

The 1980s would bring a taste of the nation's troubled times. The first violation was on 28 April 1980. That day's entry in the island visitors' book is "THE ROBBERS" – their autograph. They had left us little else. Our irritating minor losses have been to staying groups who have found it impossible to resist the pickings of an unguarded target. Every ashtray on the island – we were founded by a caucus of committed smokers – departed with a church group. The catering packs of tea-bags disappeared with a secular party. Well-intentioned tidiness has caused much grief. "You will be pleased to hear ..." my heart was already sinking ... "that the girls have burnt that awful stack of old doors."

Though we tolerated a succession of such irritations it would be our discovery by Avon Fire Service that would finally close the island to long-stay guests. The problem is one of fire precautions; to continue to operate as a self-catering hostel depended upon a certificate. That would require improvements costing £4,000 which would take up to four years to implement. As the groups staying on the island had never done much more than cover the cost of their boating and Calor gas consumption it is utterly uneconomic for a small wildlife charity to turn itself into an hotel. So the island, to our regret, has become the perquisite of a clique.

Staying visits are now restricted to members of the Kenneth Allsop Memorial Trust but day-trips can proceed almost as before. One of these, however, brought Britain's inner-city strife to the island in 1987. A group of street-wise youths who came with the *Balmoral* pleasure cruiser showed considerable skill and energy with a knife to destroy tide-flow monitoring equipment that was worth £8,000. It had been purpose-built for the island by Bidston Observatory, Merseyside, and the information was recorded on tape-spools that were also ripped apart. The attack would have passed unnoticed on the day but for a defiant last fling. A compressed-air cylinder was dropped on to the rocks, twenty feet below, and exploded with a pressure-wave that shook the boats moored off-shore. Had it been flung down at the vandals' feet it would have split their bodies.

Sometimes our achievement is in living to fight another day. On 4 June 1988 I arrived at the quayside in Weston to find the entire staff was Rose Sparrow to serve the tea, Timothy Eden to sell books and stamps, and me to fuss about everything else. Deputy warden Chris Maslen should have been there and we held the boat, when the tide was advancing to the top of the island's beach, unaware that his apology for absence had not been passed on by one of the people on the boat.

In the event the delay was merely academic for on arrival on what was left of the beach above the sea I found that my key to the island's gate had been swapped for a copy that did not fit. A request for a nail file was successful and two men worked on reshaping the key. The sea had cut us off from any other route on to the island and thirty people now had standing room only. I prepared to scale the wall to fetch a ladder, but two ladies, one without an arm and the other severely crippled, looked apprehensive.

Then the cavalry arrived, in the grey hulk of the ex-lifeboat *Lord Hurcombe*, bringing red-bearded Dr John Crothers and a group from the Field Studies Council. They coincidentally had a key, but the simultaneous arrival was both unexpected and statistically at exceedingly long odds. They had been coming to the island for years, but only once or twice in a summer, and out of our own 400 arrivals since 1978 it was just one that had previously coincided with that of the *Lord Hurcombe*.

John Crothers raised our spirits: "On Flat Holm there's a rabbit hole beside each gull nest, so I have been asking them to observe the colour variation in the rabbit eggs. It took quite some time for one of the party to ask whether it was really correct that rabbits laid eggs!"

The day had another horrific moment. As Timothy Eden finished the diminution of the offending key with a whetstone, so that we could lock the gate again, I glanced up. Above us a gull chick had fallen from the cliffs and skewered its neck on a prong of barbed wire. Mallard chicks had also been unlucky. A duck was attempting to get its brood into the sea at the moment the *Weston Lady* had landed. She had been forced to abandon them, and three limp little greenish-yellow shapes were obvious in the dull flotsam of the receding tide. Two, however, were still struggling and two girls mothered them for the day so that we could take them home to Jenny Smith, who keeps duck.

Then we had a visit from the Police launch *Signal*. Phil Russ captains her for the Marine Section of Support Division of the Avon and Somerset Constabulary. She was particularly wel-

come that day, as we were also having problems with unauthorised landers, but it did raise another problem. He brought with
him a Chief Superintendent who asked the obvious question:
"What do you do in an emergency?"

My reply: "We've a hand-portable with Zero band, which is
the Coastguards' own channel. I've been appointed an Auxiliary Coastguard for the purpose of using it, because the Department of Trade would not otherwise authorise us to have a
marine radio."

It was the truth but it concealed a greater lie – the said radio
was with the absent Chris Maslen in Bristol. For a moment we
may have needed it, as the policeman slipped on the difficult
foreshore beneath Tower Rock, but in the event the only minor
drama was with the inflatable. He had come ashore with a
young constable, Andy, and they found it tricky making the
landfall near Calf Rock. I pulled the rubber boat into a calmer
pool of water in a bowl of smooth rock immediately west of the
South Landing.

The penultimate incident of the day was that the *Weston Lady*
did not come back for us at five o'clock. In the morning the
boatmen had trouble getting off her at Weston, because of the
choppy sea. They did not come until eight o'clock when they
could return with the tide into Knightstone Causeway.
Meantime we reopened the island Barracks and gave everyone a
free cup of coffee. With an excellent pair of borrowed binoculars, Boots brand, and optically much superior to the usual
store-bought types, I identified a speck behind the Old Pier at
Birnbeck Island as our boat. She was floating, just, which was
something – and later Timmy fortuitously picked up the binoculars at Garden Battery for the moment when she moved out and
pounded into the open sea.

Lastly, after our pick-up which had most of the visitors
soaked to the knees, there came the rescue at sea. A bright blue
fishing boat had been anchored off the island all day. That was
because its engine had blown a gasket. We put a line aboard and
towed her into Weston Bay. There the rope snapped and whip-
lashed Jannis Georgiou across the cheek. He nursed a red-
dening weal for the remainder of the journey, and I suppose the
weekend.

After unloading the visitors the *Weston Lady* went out again to
resume the recovery operation. There was now the matter of
taking the Mallard chicks to Yatton. It had been a long day the
visitors would remember; sea shanties had broken out on board
during the return though nobody quite mastered Sir Henry

Newbolt's *Drake's Drum*. Four centuries before, England's little ships were gathering to fight the Spanish Armada; there will have to be a *Steep Holm Songbook* before Trafalgar goes through its bicentenary in 2005.

Steep Holm also proved a no-go area for visiting yachtsmen throughout 1988. Lydney Yacht Club had booked a visit but it was a day when only the Paul Newmans ventured into mid-channel. Just one boat remained from the flotilla, their commodore E.C. Spooner recalled, reaching "a 6 to 7 lee shore and eventually arrived back at Lydney as a drowned rat with a broken rudder".

There were many times that year when we saw proof of a seaman's truism, that rain drives down the waves, and in particular the bigger waves, by smoothing – indeed damping – the energy of wave formation. In those days Atlantic depressions moved in one after another for months on end.

Global warming then gave us entirely different weather for 1989 and 1990.

26 WESTON MERCURY, Friday, April 3, 1981.

Steep Holm trustees 'will always be hostages to weather'

ONLY by the end of 1980 had the Kenneth Allsop Memorial Trust's finances fully recovered from losses caused by the weather disrupting the 1978 Steep Holm operations, states the annual report.

"Even then they were in no better state to withstand a spate of cancelled bookings than they had been in 1978," said the report.

"It was because of the committee's awareness of this problem, that we shall always be hostages to the weather, that supportive activities were extended."

An inaugural issue of local carriage labels, coinciding with the opening of the island's own mail service, brought profits of nearly £1,000. Other sales on the island itself, particularly of food, made modest profits. The disappointment was that fewer visitors than ever were attracted by the annual report and it made a substantial loss, which absorbed by the profits arising from the book. Hardbacked book, leaving a net profit from literature sales of only £73).

The surplus for the year totalled £1,901, which was a healthy improvement upon the £1,165 surplus of the previous year. "Both years would appear more satisfactory were it not for the ...

... to a series of special filming and other facility fees.

"There were many non-profit making trips to the island for our own purposes, mainly to carry our volunteer labour force for the various building and improvement projects. A number of other exceptional and loss making visits came about as a result of a burst on the island at the beginning of the season. Insurance covered the bulk of the losses but the additional boating costs had to be borne by the Trust, and with this setback the overall surplus for the year would have been about £2,200."

The committee was relieved that subscription income, for the first time, had exceeded £1,000, and continued to grow a little faster than inflation. The collapse in the value of money caused the obsolescence of the island's guide, and it was decided that a reprint would be fashioned around a maximum wall map, to encourage the amongst visitors. "There is never enough empty wardrobe time to guarantee that people can be given conducted tours, and a more informative brochure seemed the best alternative," said the report.

Once more the guide is to include forms that explain the availability of the island for day ...

... research, the Priory ruins overlooking the beach and the Weston coast, after the simple style of a Quaker burying ground."

The archaeological section of the report says that knowledge gained from the year's work made important modifications to the gradually emerging picture of the early medieval Augustinean Priory of St. Michael.

"Probably the most significant achievement of the season was being able to discount the 1979 outline of the foundation walls as being the true proportions of the medieval priory structure." The researchers now feel that the Augustinean building was longer and wider than originally thought.

On the 1980 work produced, for the first time since the project started, a relatively large group of pottery sherds. These were 32 fragments of a tripod pitcher of gravel-tempered Devon ware, dated about 1650—"a time when there is no written record of occupation of the island."

Says the report: "There is increasing evidence of the island being occupied, or at least frequented, over the centuries, despite the apparent documentary evidence to the contrary."

The outstanding Roman find of the 1980 was that of a large piece of amphora. It was ...

OPPOSITE:

Hands to the rope: *Ivanhoe* washed broadsides on to the beach on Steep Holm. It only survived this incident because of its steel-plated hull. Seen from the west. Photographed by Mike Webber in 1980.

Washed away: Rodney Legg swept off his feet from the bows of the *Ivanhoe*, instantly recognisable from his rags (far right). Seen from the west. Photographed by Mike Webber in 1980.

Island of birds 'killed by poison'

by Mark Ellis

SCIENTISTS are investigating why an island once teeming with birdlife is now almost deserted. Steep Holm in the Bristol Channel used to be home to one of Britain's largest herring gull colonies; today it juts into the sky, silent and grey.

A rare pair of peregrine falcons has disappeared, and now even the ravens have gone. The 50-acre sanctuary, five miles off Weston-super-Mare, has no human inhabitants and is protected by 250ft limestone cliffs which once echoed to the calls of gulls.

"It is a silent island — eerie because you could not hear yourself talk above the raucous shrieks of 10,000 pairs of gulls, while now there are just 200 pairs," said Rodney Legg, island warden, yesterday.

Dead and dying birds are being examined by biologists at Cardiff University. One theory is that they are the latest victims of food poisoning, dying of botulism from scavenging from household dustbin bags on tips. Pollution from industrial discharges into the Severn Estuary is another possible cause.

Bodies of herring gulls litter the island, with chicks abandoned in nests to starve. Many lesser black-backed gulls, listed recently as one of Europe's threatened birds, have also vanished. Peregrine falcons, which bred on the island

Bodies on the beaches: Rodney Legg, warden on Steep Holm, finds only dead herring gulls on an island once teeming with wildlife

every year for a decade, did not return this year.

The peregrines are the emblem of the trust, which bought the island in 1976 as a memorial to Kenneth Allsop, the journalist and naturalist, three years after his death.

Legg, secretary of the Kenneth Allsop Memorial Trust, said: "The ecology of the island is falling apart and, because of its location, it must

be a barometer of the environmental health of the nation.

"We are told by the authorities there is less pollution, but it is a particularly filthy piece of water, and all the fishermen complain that catches are nothing like those in the past."

Ten years ago 10,000 breeding pairs of herring gulls used every available inch of the island to nest, including Victorian gun batteries and the

remains of a 13th-century priory. Some visitors left in tears because they found it impossible to walk around without standing on chicks or eggs.

A count yesterday found just 200 pairs, and only one in four had bred successfully, showing that the decline was accelerating, according to Legg.

He said there had also been a large hedgehog population,

but that too had been blighted. "I think the food chain has broken down and the island is becoming a hostile environment for wildlife."

Herring gulls have been found with the symptoms of botulism — listlessness and drooping wings – as the toxin paralyses their nervous system.

Dr Peter Ferns, senior lecturer in biology at Cardiff

University, is working [on a] paper to show a link [between] botulism from household waste and herring gull [...]

The decline of the gull coincided with [in]troduction in the mid [...] plastic dustbin bags [...] sealed they create an [air]tight breeding ground [...] strain of botulism [...] clostridium botulinum [...] in turn produced toxi[n] to gulls.

"What we have n[ot estab]lished is where they [come] from, but I am fairly c[ertain] it is from refuse tips [...] still collecting corpses [for do]ing corpse counts," sa[id ...]

The trust is re-rou[ting the] main path on the [...] which attracts thousa[nds of] bird-watchers and wa[ders] every summer, awa[y from] clifftops to encourage [fal]cons to return to their [...]

Allsop's widow, B[etty] said: "What is happe[ning to] the island worries me [...] it is a reflection of [what is] happening to the worl[d ...]

Peregrines were a [great] passion for Allsop, wh[o wrote] a letter to his wife fro[m Steep Holm] shortly before his de[ath say]ing: "The tiercel (mal[e ...] and falcon when the[y ...] up into the bright sk[y ...] those tumbling dive[s over] the crags, free spirits, [...] right, and everything [that] we represented – o[ne] which poisons the [...] shoots them and ste[als ...] eggs and young – se[...] We are the predators [...] ers, not those peregri[nes ...]

Botulism: cartoon by Paice in the Bristol Evening Post. 'Death on Bird Island' headlined the Western Daily Press that morning, 7 August 1989.

Arrival of botulism

Steep Holm heated up as much as anywhere in the record temperatures of 1989, the hottest year on record, but its problems came from off the island. Botulism, the toxic muscular paralysis that is the most lethal form of food poisoning, caused the almost total demise of the herring gull, which had never recovered in numbers from similar outbreaks in the previous record summers of 1975-76. They caused the collapse of Steep Holm as one of the greatest gulleries on the western seaboard.

Back in the spring of 1975 there were 10,000 pairs of herring gull nesting on the island in every available spot, as well as some that were not – such as between the tide-lines. By June the population, with clutches of three chicks per nest, reached 50,000 birds. Then the beach, cliffs and paths were littered with thousands of dead gulls of all ages. Hot-house conditions dried and mummified the victims as the odour of decomposing corpses drifted far out to sea.

At first the deaths were thought to be caused by dehydration and the natural losses of an exceedingly large colony. Then Cardiff University researchers took off several sacks of carcasses. They diagnosed avian type-C botulism.

Being a scavenger, which these days means a tip-feeder, the gulls were picking up the virulent bacterium from fragments of food putrifying at high temperatures in the relatively newly introduced micro-conditions of sealed plastic rubbish sacks.

As Alan Blythe, Woodspring's director of environmental health, later explained to me: "Aerobic organisms quickly exhaust the available oxygen and lead to conditions where anaerobes like *clostridia* species can thrive."

The herring gull colony was estimated at between 500 and 600 pairs at the end of the 1988 breeding season. Most of these birds would succumb to disease during the prolonged hot weather of 1989.

This time the climate of public opinion and stories of pollution and food hygiene could be newsworthy. "POISON THREAT TO BIRD ISLAND" was the front-page headline in the Western Daily Press of 18 May. "Pollution link with missing herring gulls" the Sunday Telegraph reported on 21 May. "Falcons flee island nest" was the Western Daily Press story of 4 August that gave the news that for the first time in the 1980s, Peregrines had failed to breed. "Nature island crisis as birds fly away" the Bristol Evening Post continued that evening, reporting instances of human disturbance adding to the plight of the birds.

"Island of birds 'killed by poison'," wrote Mark Ellis in the Sunday Times of 6 August, bringing botulism into the story and quoting Dr Peter Ferns, senior lecturer in biology at Cardiff University, saying that the decline in the Herring Gulls had coincided with the introduction of plastic dustbin liners. "When sealed they create an ideal air-tight breeding ground for a strain of botulism bacteria, clostridium botulism, which in turn produced toxins fatal to the gulls," Ellis explained.

Kenneth Allsop's widow, Betty, told him: "What is happening on the island worries me because it is a reflection of what is happening to the world."

On 5 August the Allsop Trust's annual meeting heard that during the course of the day veterinary surgeon Tony Parsons had confirmed for the first time that gull-brought island botulism had moved sideways, via infected food, to other species. The island's pair of Magpies had been picked up freshly dead, without any sign of anything being wrong with them – the classic botulism scenario.

"Death on Bird Island" the Western Daily Press proclaimed on 7 August. That story made a cartoon for Paice, with the paper lying on the island beach beside dead birds and a skull and crossbones hazard sign "STEEP HOLM – VICTIM OF THE CONSUMER SOCIETY."

The Western Daily Press editorial for 7 August was ringing in its denouncement of the problem: "The cause of the disaster is no less alarming. It is chilling to believe that so much wildlife has been destroyed by the simple use of domestic dustbin liners, but it brings us face to face with a new ecological consequence of the Effluent Society.

"That plastic binliners, which were introduced in the name of hygiene, should have proved such a powerful incubator for deadly avian botulism is an irony that cannot be lost on conservationists."

"The Island of Death" was the spread across the centre pages of the Western Daily Press of 15 September, with Chris Rundle's sub-heading being "Sanctuary that's now the place where birds fly home to perish".

An equally tragic aside to the bird news of 1989 was the arrival of two of the largest and most colourful birds ever to be seen on Steep Holm. One morning in July I descended the steps from the top of the island and turned the corner into the sycamore wood, to find myself mobbed by two Military Macaws. These spectacular birds have vivid green bodies, red heads and blue tails.

"They commandeered our only trees and came out to squawk at me," I told the Bristol Evening Post on 21 July. "Our gull colony went mad and trying to feed the macaws with water melon was a failure."

The headline told the most of the story: "Rare bird dies of hunger on island."

The birds came from Australia and were the pride and joy of their Somerset owner, Mrs Stella Peacock. "There are only four pairs of Military Macaws in Britain, and imports have been banned as they are an endangered species," the Western Daily Press wrote on 5 August, reporting a sighting of the dead bird's mate being forced down to sea-level by a mob of gulls.

It managed to fly to the Exmoor coast but died from exhaustion on arrival. Both bodies were returned to Mrs Peacock at her request, for burial at Widcombe Tropical Bird Gardens, near Wellington, Somerset, from where they had escaped after pecking their way out of their cage.

Early next summer, botulism was back and the Western Daily Press of 30 May 1990 headed the story:

"Botulism kills island's rare gulls."

Herring gulls were now down to a hundred pairs and outnumbered something like four or five to one by the fish-feeding Lesser Black-backed Gulls.

Over the hot Spring holiday weekend two out of the three chicks had died in a nest at just about the coolest spot on the island, behind iron girders between the boathouse and the eastern cliffs, despite parental tending. Dehydration in this case seemed unlikely, even if it was a major cause of chick deaths elsewhere on the island.

Global warming was turning botulism into an annual occurrence, given the link between the disease and air temperature. Once again I tried to emphasise that it was not an island problem but one imported to it from mainland rubbish tips: "The only answer to it is for people to stop using black plastic sacks, but that's like demanding that we disinvent the motor car."

Demonstrative: Heinz Sielmann, the first to film intimate wildlife programmes in the nest, at 70. He had just successfully achieved his ambition of 'imprinting' a new-born gull chick, for German television. Seen in the Barracks on Steep Holm. Photographed by Rodney Legg on 6 June 1989.

Heinz Sielmann films our gulls

The doyen of wildlife film-makers Heinz Sielmann, at the age of seventy, flew across from Hamburg to film the gull colony on Steep Holm at what turned out to be the peak of the botulism epidemic. He came with Uwe Schmidt, the nature unit manager of Norddeutscher Deutschland Rundfunk, one of Germany's main television stations, and teamed up with the London film crew of Rick Manzanero, Ben Hodgson and Ron Crabb to sail in the *Weston Lady* for Steep Holm on Tuesday 6 June 1989.

They had not intended shooting harrowing footage of dead or dying birds but to capture the behavioural patterns of healthy ones. In that they would be successful, as Evan Williams reported for the Burnham and Highbridge Weekly News: "The day's filming included Heinz standing on the cliff edge against a background of wheeling gulls, kneeling beside nests and being dive-bombed by irate parents, and conducting instinctive reflex-action experiments on chicks, using model gull heads to demonstrate the chicks' reaction to the red bill spot which, when tapped by the youngster, operates a release mechanism and makes the parents regurgitate food."

It had long been Sielmann's ambition to carry out "imprinting" and he was delighted to have fooled at least one chick into thinking he was its parent. "It works!" he beamed. As for the species of baby bird, no one mentioned that they were Lesser Black-backed youngsters rather than the intended Herring Gull offspring.

Two nests of the latter had been earmarked by me for the filming three days before, on the Saturday. They were conveniently placed, five feet apart, so that the crew could have an alternative shot lined-up in the event of non-cooperation from the first nest. The nests were on a remnant of the island's once extensive eastern gull-lawn and had amiable parents who seemed ambivalent to human disturbance. None swooped on me as I reconnoitred the situation. These were the only surviving herring gulls in an area otherwise dominated by the now much commoner Lesser Black-backed Gulls.

There had been more Herring Gulls, who owned the scattering of empty or deserted nests, and some of their bodies were lying at the edge of the clearing beside the Alexander stalks.

On returning to the spot, ahead of the film crew on the Tuesday, I was dismayed to find that one of the chosen nests was occupied by two dead chicks. The other had a freshly dead Herring Gull draped across it. The wings were still limp, half-stretched, with no outward sign of disease or damage anywhere on the body, in what was a classic case of clostridium collapse. These gulls had scavenged some botulism over the weekend.

It was impossible to find alternative Herring Gull nests. As I wasted time trying to locate some, Heinz Sielmann decided that instead he would film the almost identical chicks of the similar-sized Lesser Black-backed Gulls.

These proved to be a perfect substitute and the average central European viewer would never know the difference when the NDR production went out at 20.15 hours on 16 August 1989.

It was time to relax with claret and lager in the Barracks. Heinz regaled us with the story of his experiences in South Georgia, on leaving the Penguins and Elephant Seals to cross the island from west to east via the glaciers of Mount Paget and search out the descent to the old whaling station at Grytviken.

"You weren't the first to do that!" I interjected, dismissively, to reproachful glances from the rest of the party. "I think the others were pulling their boat."

"He knows, he knows," Heinz winked. "He knows the story."

It was a reference to Sir Ernest Shackleton's epic journey for help after the *Endurance* had been crushed by the Antarctic ice in 1916.

There was further praise for my picture-taking, on a borrowed Canon Sureshot. "You watch him, you can learn from him," Heinz told Uwe Schmidt, who showed no sign of wanting or needing such advice and was probably considering a reply in German. "The angle," Heinz went on. "He keeps moving until he has the angle right! See the angles he chooses."

My embarrassment that day was the rushed printing of *Steep Holm Wildlife*, written with Tony Parsons, which had been hurriedly dedicated to Heinz so that we could present him with the first copy. That task was carried out admirably by Timothy Eden, the Trust's youngest member, but I then found I had misspelt Sielmann. That was despite, or rather because of, a letter from the BBC, organising the trip, received a month before. At the time I realised it might be wrong and phoned the natural history unit in Bristol to check; only to be assured that their spelling was correct.

"We might as well give up if we can't even get people's names right," a BBC reporter told me when they had done the same to mine, years before on the nine o'clock news. "Or something like that!" I used to mutter when Reginald Bosanquet slurred yet another name on the other channel.

120

My sanity this day was saved by a series of chuckles with Karen Eden, mother of Timmy and now remarried to Richard Wike, on the theme of "The Germans". They were inspired by Weston-born John Cleese and *Fawlty Towers*: "Don't mention the war!" It was particularly relevant because we leapt ashore with our Germans on the morning of the 45th anniversary of the D-Day landings. I had at least left my Sten-gun at home.

Heinz concluded with a message that the plight of the planet had been deteriorating at a rate of knots since his classic production of 1955, *Woodpeckers – Carpenters of the Forest*, which was shown in this country on Peter Scott's "Look" series at a time when the BBC still had the only television channel. Now, Heinz emphasised, the problem had progressed from endangered wildlife into a global malaise threatening the existence of mankind as well.

"We are only a link in the chain of life," he explained. "Like every other creature we need fresh air and clean water. The increase in the human population is making excessive demands on Mother Nature and in the end she will repay."

Back with the flood: homeward from Steep Holm on a rising tide at evening, though still with Calf Rock out of the water (left) and the island in profile. John Watts and Pete Holder are in the wheelhouse of *Weston Lady*. Standing, with folded arms, are Stan Rendell (left) and John (Kenny) Watts senior. Seen from the east. Photographed by Colin Graham in 1982.

Steps swept away

Paradoxically, in between glorious summers the incidence of very high winds increased dramatically. A possible explanation for the increasing frequency of violent weather is that rising temperatures – for example the 0.6 degree Celcius rise in Atlantic sea-surface values at the end of summer in 1990 compared with those for the same time in 1989 – are creating the storm energetics that power the devastating winds that have been tracking across the British Isles, instead of following their traditional course further to the north. They used to pass harmlessly across the Faroe Islands and generally blew over without comment. When such winds come south it is a different matter.

Speeds in excess of 100 miles per hour swept across the West Country towards lunchtime on Thursday 25 January 1990 but there had been only a 10.5 metre tide, and that had been at 05.45 hours, so by mid-morning the water level was well down the beach.

On Monday 26 February 1990 things were very different. Though the wind speed was lower, at 80 miles per hour, it coincided with high water at Weston-super-Mare and this time it was a big tide, predicted as 12.4 metres at 07.21 hours. In fact, at eight o'clock, it was 1.75 metres higher than forecast, with great waves that tore huge gashes in the sea wall along Weston promenade and smashed the landing steps on Steep Holm. There it also burst open the iron gates with its pressure and surged at waist height through the boathouse and into the first room above the steps at the Inn.

The island ferryboat, the *Weston Lady*, was in theory out of the water at the time, on a trolley beside the promenade, but she refloated as Weston flooded and bobbed about above the seaside seats and canopies before being ripped apart in the vicinity of the Winter Gardens. Though the flagship had been lost, another vessel in Frank Watts's fleet, the much smaller *Silver Spray*, rode out the storm at anchor off Knightstone Causeway.

Faced with the prospect of limited capacity for trips for the rest of the season, the second blow for the island's finances was the discovery that the steps were unsuitable for use by ordinary visitors, who are already ahead of their time in demographic

OPPOSITE:
Chasm: the steps beside the island's only landing beach were washed away by a big tide that combined with high winds, reaching a record for the day at 92 miles per hour over Leeds. *Weston Lady* was shipwrecked at eight o'clock that morning, 26 February 1990. Rodney Legg holds a dead seagull. Seen from the south-east with the equally battered gates in the background. Photographed by John Pitfield in March 1990.

mix and generally include a number of "active elderly". Though the front of the steps had survived, all the back part had been washed out, and the central section projected over a chasm into a metre-wide gap.

There was to be more bad news. On the mainland, Elizabeth Fowles was seriously ill, "invaded by a brutally rapid form of cancer". It was not diagnosed as such until 21 February 1990, and she died on the evening of 1 March. John Fowles expressed it poignantly at a time when words are always inadequate: "She left this life with a minimum of fuss; as gracefully as she once danced, as smoothly and quickly as a dabchick dives under water. I am left a good deal less than even half a never very whole human being. Please let Eliz stay in your memory. Such is the only life after death."

Poor John; she was not merely his helpmate and protector but a marvellously complementary presence who excelled in all those pleasantries and practicalities an occasion demanded. We could always chuckle over the latest string of problems from "that bloody island" and on my wall from 1976 is Liz's "Dear Rodders" card from "le pittoresque village de Gourdon" on la Cote d'Azur, featuring cliff-edge architecture of the sort I have since attempted for the beach-side wardening depot that has arisen from the ruins of the Inn on Steep Holm.

"This is my idea for rebuilding the barracks at Steep Holm," she wrote. "Let committee members know. Actually driving round and round these bloody mountains is only slightly less terrifying, for me, than that damned Bristol Channel crossing."

Colin Graham used to say he thought it quite likely that it was Elizabeth who wrote the books. John had long ago moved on from the routine difficulties that island chairmanship entailed to life presidency of the Allsop Trust. Without the Fowleses (a less awkward plural than it sounds) we could never have bought Steep Holm nor started its stewardship with such a great sense of fun. Liz would have found it ironic to be leaving us as our ferry was shipwrecked and landing point swept away by a hurricane.

The island had to be closed for repairs to take place, during which Chris Maslen directed the efforts of teams from RAF Locking and Clevedon Auxiliary Coastguards, helped by Wood-spring District Council chief executive Bob Moon who chan-nelled his energy into hard labour as retirement neared. The most disconcerting part of the job was that having exposed the foundations, the sea then pushed tons of pebbles into the hole.

These had to be removed before work could start. Much of

the surviving part of the structure had then to be destroyed in order to replace material in the recesses beneath.

As work proceeded, cautious eyes noticed that the vibration was loosening boulders on the overhanging cliff above. Chris Maslen prised them off with a bar as he swung in space from the end of a ladder. Ironically, the ones that looked dangerous had been perfectly safe, and needed considerable effort to free, but others that appeared sound dropped off with little more than a touch. Some were between two and three hundredweight. They joined the hardcore below.

When the sea returned to the top of the beach and the island's beleaguered access point it was on its best behaviour. The next round of high spring tides splashed harmlessly around the debris without contributing more damage.

The finale was the loan of a military helicopter for the morning of Friday 11 May 1990 to drop five tons of sand and cement among gull nests on the only patch of open ground at the top of the cliffs. RAF Odiham expected to send a twin-rotor Chinook from the Hampshire Downs, but in the event it was a Puma that approached from Brean Down, coming over the sea with its landing light on and the first of four loads underslung in a net. It looked impressive enough and all plopped down on cue.

Despite the frenetic activity, observed by the cameras of three rival television stations, no eggs were broken. When everyone had departed, leaving me alone to grapple with tarpaulins in a squall, the gulls commandeered the new observation posts and each pile of sacks had its sentinels, diffident about this latest outbreak of mad human disease as they watched me struggle, ignoring the stones I was tossing to within a few feet of them to hold down the covers.

Next day the wind dropped and the people returned, notably Caroline, Duchess of Beaufort, as the island reopened to its public. Their only disappointment was with the wild peony, the island's famous monastic introduction, because the only petals they saw were on the ground. As with just about every plant in Britain it had flowered a month early.

Down at the beach Bob Moon declared "the Maslen Steps" open, with wine and thanks to the RAF.

The Maslen Steps: named and toasted by Bob Moon (foreground, right) in tribute to
Chris Maslen who did much of the work (seated, centre). Lads and ladies of the Royal
Air Force, from the radar school at Locking, line up behind. Stan Rendell sits on the
left. Seen from the east. Photographed by Rodney Legg in May 1990.

Severn Tidal Energy Barrage

Continuing the theme of the power of the sea, the island is destined for a close encounter with the Severn Tidal Energy Barrage if it is ever built.

The exceptional geography of semi-landlocked stretches of water facing the open sea, as with the Severn Estuary, creates funnelling of the tides, and remarkable differences of level between the lowest of ebb tides and the highest spring flows. The difference is 14 to 15 metres in the Severn, and it is often said to have the greatest tide-range in the world, though Ungara Bay in Canada can manage more than 16 metres.

With these facts in mind, plus the marked psychological and practical turn towards consideration of and investment in the ways of using natural energy – given the impetus of dwindling fossil fuels and the dread of the plutonium alternative – it is regarded by many as likely that the Severn tide-flow will eventually be harnessed. The estuary has a three million population near its shores, and the concept of an electricity generating hydrotidal scheme is attractive. Already, pilot experiments on a small scale at La Rance in Brittany have been successful and provided the necessary expertise and experience.

One of the most seriously considered plans proposed a 15-mile dam across the conveniently shallow waters of the Bristol Channel from Brean Down to the Welsh coast, incorporating both Steep Holm and Flat Holm on the way. Not that the idea is new to Britain. Ramsay MacDonald's cabinet approved a feasibility study into the possibilities of a Severn barrage on 9 July 1924. The study group was set up in 1925 and reported in 1933. This country was then closer to its age of great construction works. The Dutch are always credited with the ability to build dams with apparent ease, but a length of breakwater equal to that necessary to dam the Severn was built in England in the nineteenth century, across far deeper water, to make a four-square-mile harbour refuge at Portland.

There is unlikely to be just a simple barrier across the Bristol Channel as that would too narrowly restrict the number of hours during which the scheme would be capable of producing power. As well as the main dam, a large holding reservoir – to capture some of the surging water and stagger its release – would be necessary. The water would spin turbines to produce the power, at a construction cost estimated at between three and four billion pounds by a government report in 1977. Subsequent increases in the estimated costs are balanced, if not exceeded, by inflationary pressures on the value of the electricity it would provide.

The prospects of Steep Holm being physically destroyed as a quarry for these dams was mentioned at a seminar packed with envoys from the nation's construction industry, held on 7 September 1977. Dr Tom Shaw of Bristol University told Tony Benn, the Secretary of State for Energy: "It is easy and dangerous to draw lines on a map. The impression is given that the barrage needs to hang on to Steep Holm. I shudder when I see my name attached to something driving through Steep Holm."

In 1980 the Department of Energy's chief scientist, Sir Hermann Bondi, declared the project to be technically feasible. His committee selected two possible lines for the Severn Barrage – one far to the west of the island, near Minehead, and the other from Lavernock Point to Sand Point, a mile to the north of Steep Holm. The latter route was preferred. "The flood tide would be allowed through the sluices into the upper estuary and then forced to flow back through power-generating turbines on the ebb," David Fairhall reported in The Guardian of 6 March 1980. The project was "on the brink of being economically competitive without the physical hazards of nuclear power or the political problems of oil and coal supply". This strategic power source, as others were now calling it, was said to be capable of meeting five per cent of Britain's electricity demand.

"No definite barrage site, type of barrage or method of working has yet been chosen," Sir Hermann Bondi assured me. "Even further away are the details of engineering which would enable me to be definite about how the island of Steep Holm is likely to lie in relation to a finally proposed barrage.

"I can assure you, however, that my committee is strongly concerned with the environmental and general visual impact of a barrage and is unlikely to countenance any cavalier disregard for the amenity you hold in trust."

That was left to the media and a number of pundits from the quasi-governmental service industries who floated like a froth around the school halls and exhibition centres of Avon and Somerset. In the Weston Mercury of 4 April 1980 I denounced "the trivial and sloppy presentation that passes as 'news' in the two Bristol television studios. The media persist in showing old maps and models of past routes that were never more than tentative suggestions, and which have since been eliminated as unsatisfactory" – these were schemes, a Dutch one in particular, that incorporated Steep Holm in the dam wall. That would have taken up valuable turbine space. Some took it a stage further and showed the island as a quarry, without giving much consideration to the problems of operating a stone mine in the middle of the sea; and all were yesterday's ideas. "We are victims of a classic example of planning blight, but it is a threat that is imagined rather than real," I went on. "It is a myth of the media."

In 1987 I was still trying to make the same point. "What's happening about the Barrage?" had become a perennial question. Misinformation, such as the bending of the plans to suggest the elimination of the island, continued to be disseminated. In fact the current favourite was the upper of the 1980 lines but it had shifted westward a little, from Sand Point to the west side of Brean Down, from where an access road for construction traffic would be built to the M5. From here it passed over the South Patches, with a line of 105 sluices being proposed, and was then proposed to pass half a mile north of the island – leaving Steep Holm in the open sea – with its battery of 192 turbines being placed in mid-channel to the north of Rudder Rock. There would then be a further 81 sluices, a shipping lock, and a landfall between Sully Island and Lavernock Point. Feasibility studies are continuing and a drilling rig has confirmed, as everyone expected, that the seabed is uninterrupted limestone.

If it does become more than an academic exercise, in the light of a post-privatisation power industry, the environmental concerns will be as complex as the engineering. Ecologically, the upper Bristol Channel is going to become a different kind of marine environment – one in which blue waters will return as the lessened tide-flow causes the sea to drop its sediment.

Blue or green, the present hazardous waters would become immediately attractive to masses of yachts and small boats, in the sort of density that plagues Poole Harbour. With this prospect of lasting ecological conflict, the birds are going to need Steep Holm even more than they do at the moment, and it can become the one practical symbol of stability in a transformed environment. Its greatest threat may come not from the dam builders themselves, who can be manipulated via public inquiries, letters to The Times and deputations to Whitehall, but from the inevitable pressures brought about by increase in leisure appeal.

Such changes could hardly be compatible with the present use of the Bristol Channel as an open sewer. Industrial pollutants from the northern shoreline, and Bristol itself, are the most obvious threats to the purity of the water, plus an emergency pipeline for radioactive waste from the Hinkley Point reactors, and a weekly tanker service from the Avon to discharge the conurbation's sewage. This vessel usually dumps its load downstream from Steep Holm, but on 20 May 1977 it emptied only a mile south-east of the island.

The work of Professor Heinz Kaminski of Bochum Observatory in West Germany, using infra-red photographs taken by United States NDAA environmental satellites, shows that the Bristol Channel is one of the five British estuaries where thermal radiation data suggests there is little water exchange with the deeper sea. Kaminski warns that shallow waters of this type remain stable throughout the year, and are at extreme risk from pollutants, because waste matter flowing down rivers and discharged from the shore is not dispersed into the open sea but remains in the inshore zone. The Bristol Channel, for its entire length east of Lundy, comes into that category and is included in Kaminski's diagrams of "the environmentally sick areas of Europe".

The Kenneth Allsop Memorial Trust has been pragmatic. We have promised to co-operate with the barrage scheme provided it does not damage the island or cut us off from our mainland ferry base at Weston. Unfortunately, in the revised line being considered in 1991, that is just what is going to happen if the barrage is ever built.

With each refinement of the scheme the line of the proposed barrage has edged closer to the island, and the latest map shows it having impacted with the north-east corner of Steep Holm. Sub-stations number one and two will be on a 30-acre platform set at an angle to the island, extending to the north-west and the south-east. Either side there are breakwaters with 168 turbine generators to the north-west of Steep Holm and another group of 48 turbines to the south-east. The island is well within sight and sound of the barrage; and smell as well if a dual carriageway is added on top as the "bolt-on optional extra". Less attention has been paid to the needs of yachts and motor-boats as their only lock is shown on the south-west tip of Brean Down in a rocky and turbulent piece of water which boatmen do their best to avoid. The current line would be a disaster for the island.

It will leave us out in the open sea but cut off from our lifeline to Weston-super-Mare. Providing us with a closer "small craft lock" will solve nothing.

Every year there are occasions when the sea is flat calm when we go across to the island in the morning, but by the evening a strengthening south-westerly is blowing; and lifting people off the island can be a close-run thing. The water can go from a mill pond to massive waves in a matter of hours.

In those conditions there is no way our boat is going to be able to negotiate the double gauntlet of coming out of the safe water behind the barrage into a rising sea and then returning through it with passengers. Approaching lock gates and being pushed by a gale we would be liable to be swept into the immense concrete wall and smashed up beside the turbines.

The solution I have been advocating is for a low water causeway across the half mile of sea that will separate Steep Holm from the barrage. That would be similar to the picturesque cobbled strand that attaches St Michael's Mount to the Cornish mainland. For twenty hours a day it would be covered by the sea and Steep Holm would remain an island.

Jet-skis and other misadventures

The beach off Steep Holm is an accident waiting to happen. During the tropical Spring holiday weekend in 1990 a swimmer came back from it describing "several hairy minutes swimming against the current and staying in the same place". The tide had turned in the course of what had started out as a paddle. The point was chosen for the laying of tide-flow monitors in the 1980s for the very reason that it showed signs of powerful mid-channel tidal surges.

Likewise that Whitsun the tide-race across the pebbles off the island's eastern beach provided an unexpected moment of excitement for parties of jet-skiers who had come across in mill pond conditions from Weston-super-Mare. The police launch *Signal* encountered another flotilla of these potentially unstable craft in the shipping lane off Clevedon.

"You have to have a good sense of balance," said one of the fair-weather sailors as he relaunched himself towards the mainland with defiant S-shaped twists and turns.

That weekend the unauthorised landers totalled twenty-three and their craft also included canoes, power-boats, yachts and a fishing boat.

Much of the interest is born of boredom on Weston seafront. When you are floating off Weston sands with a lilo and a paddle, looking across at Steep Holm is the ultimate challenge – it's the equivalent of climbing Everest. Some people have even contemplated walking to Steep Holm and the same spirit of misadventure has caused drownings in the River Axe, with walkers trying to wade across the estuary to Brean Down.

Three men in a boat were rescued three times off Steep Holm during the weekend of 14 July 1990. The misadventurers put their seven-foot inflatable dinghy on the roof-rack of a car in Redland, Bristol, on the Friday afternoon and launched it into the sea at Clevedon. They had no prior idea of the state of the tide, which they soon found was going out – enabling them to make 20 knots headway for much of their twelve mile journey down the estuary to Steep Holm. None of them wore a wet-suit or a life-jacket, and they had no two-way radio or distress flares.

Disaster almost struck off Steep Holm when the fuel-line into the outboard motor became disconnected in a heavy swell. They found themselves sucked into the island's tide-race and went round in circles, using only a single paddle, as the inside of the rubber boat became swamped.

"Why have you only got one paddle?" I asked as I helped

them ashore. "The other dropped off the roof of the car a couple of weeks ago," was the reply.

The three were in their early twenties. I persuaded them not to attempt the return journey at dusk but to stay overnight in the island's emergency bunks.

They were Simon Colburn, Andy Burdock and Pete Cheacker. I took a note of their parents' telephone numbers and radioed Swansea Coastguard so that messages could be relayed to their homes, to say they were safe and staying on Steep Holm for the night.

In the morning things went from bad to worse. The island's ferry, *Silver Spray*, was due out with a party of visitors, and I said she could tow them back to the mainland. Instead they departed in the dinghy, before I realised they were going and whilst still owing payment for a bottle of wine. The incoming tide was in their favour but the engine failed again.

Fortunately it did so beside a blue fishing boat, *Weston Boy*, which happened to be about the only craft anywhere in sight. She responded to their cries for help and towed them back to within a hundred yards of the island. They splashed about as the tide pushed them towards the pebbles.

"Simon – how nice of you to paddle back to pay me!" I had been rehearsing that line for half-an-hour.

Pete Cheacker refused to contemplate a further voyage and walked off to look at the plants and the birds. The other two, again turning down the prospect of returning in the *Silver Spray* an hour later, insisted on making a third attempt to leave.

Pete and I watched as their movement stopped a mile and a half or so off the island, beyond the South Patches sandbank, and I radioed Ashleigh Holtby and John Watts who were coming out of Weston Bay in the *Silver Spray*. I gave the position of the dinghy, which was drifting up-Channel with the tide, and the two specks gradually converged. Then Ashleigh spotted them: "We have them visually."

The two men were completely soaked by the time they were pulled from their rubber boat, which was then towed back to the island by the *Silver Spray*. She returned them, plus the third man, to Weston where they were met by a Coastguard Land-rover and given an ear-bending.

It was a close-run thing. If the three of them had gone on the third attempt then one at least would have drowned as they were completely swamped. But I can't keep people on the island by force and you cannot legislate against stupidity, though you can prepare for the eventuality.

Island graveyard

"Tombstone with a view" was one of the newspaper headlines after the Trust decided to allow urn burials on Steep Holm, in an extension to the graveyard of the mediaeval monks.

Members were upset at the Trust's annual meeting in 1990 that we might have had a flood of applicants. In fact there were only two, and those had been on the books for several years. It was also explained that there would be no open-ended responsibility for looking after graves in perpetuity; just for fifty years, so as not to burden our successors.

There would be a prohibition on exotica like weeping angels or plastic flowers, and the rabbits and Muntjac deer would put conventional floral tributes straight into the food chain. The memorial would be restricted to a simple stone a foot square, flat with the ground, which would be just the right size to provide a home-base for a gull nest.

The meeting was fussed that because I had drafted a burial application form, outsiders would apply. They thought that island burial was a privilege and were openly elitist about it: long-standing members only will be allowed. Bodies have to be refused, for the practical reason that the island is a solid lump of rock with barely two inches of soil. Access problems for live visitors apply equally to cremated ones. They are warned, on the application form, that their funeral arrangements will have to fit in with the weather, subject to postponement if they coincide with an Atlantic depression belting up the Bristol Channel.

The island's primary role remains as a nature reserve – not a burial ground – though having said that, the two can be mutually compatible, as with the disused Victorian cemeteries that are the best wildlife sanctuaries in London and many other major cities.

Burial deal for island lovers

WESTERN MAIL

With Compliments

Ziki becomes
Baroness Wharton

How on earth can one congratulate someone on their Barony when it is one of the oldest in existence, with half a millennium of pedigree? Conveniently coinciding with my recording for posterity of her part in the virtual giving of the island of Steep Holm to the Kenneth Allsop Memorial Trust Limited, I heard that Myrtle Olive Felix Robertson, the Honourable Mrs Henry McLeod Robertson, was henceforth the eleventh Baroness Wharton, the title – created in 1544-45 – having been called out of abeyance in 1990.

Ziki, as she is known, has taken her seat as a cross-bencher in the House of Lords and spoken on animal welfare issues for the RSPCA. Born on 20 February 1934, the daughter of David George Arbuthnot who died in 1985, and Baroness Wharton, she has three sons and a daughter. Her heir is the Honourable Myles Christopher David Robertson who was born on 1 October 1964.

I think of them disturbingly often, whenever I hear the family refrain, lillibullero, which happens to be the introductory tune to "This is London" – the hourly news throughout the night on the BBC World Service.

Oiled waters

We tend to exaggerate worries about the effect on wildlife of sporadic instances of human interference. What does upset the balance and survival of nature is the tide of filth with which it has to contend. In the prolonged frosts of early February in 1991 a pipe fractured at the British Steel works at Llanwern, near Newport, and twenty tons of fuel oil leaked into the Bristol Channel.

For several days it sloshed up and down mid-Channel, backwards and forwards past the island, but on Steep Holm itself we found only negative evidence. There was no oil but there were few birds.

The oil had been there – we watched the National Rivers Authority launch picking up specimens of oil-soaked debris – but apart from spotty flecks it had largely been scoured from the island's rocks. That was hardly surprising, given the location in the middle of an exceedingly fast tide-race.

When we left Weston our boat, *Silver Spray*, had a two inch band of oil as a plimsoll line. By the time we arrived off the island it had washed off.

People imagine that oiled birds are easily rescued, washed and returned to the wild. In this emergency they had that impression reinforced by television pictures of oiled birds being gathered up in blankets from Portishead and sent down the motorway to the RSPCA wildlife hospital at West Hatch, near Taunton. A swan was the star casualty.

In practice, on the island, things do not work out like that. Each year we spot the occasional oiled cormorant that has found an unreported discharge. Once Chris Maslen, Jenny Smith and myself went in hot pursuit of one totally oiled bird but it managed to hop ahead of us from rock pool to outcrop as we staggered around the deeply fissured fringes of the northern cliffs and eventually had to abandon the exercise and rescue ourselves from the turning of the tide.

Things were no different in the February spill. Though spared harrowing encounters in close-up that left us feeling helpless we were inadequate for doing more than merely monitoring the situation. Cormorant numbers were well down, it being difficult to reach forty on the ledges where the previous October we had counted over a hundred birds. Some seemed to be oiled but with black birds, a hundred feet above us, it was hard to feel sure.

On the southern side of the island the presence of the impressive Great Black-backed Gulls, usually so noticeable and in the region of thirty or more, had diminished to only six.

Herring Gulls on Steep Holm are already much reduced in number due to recurrent outbreaks of botulism but some of the one hundred or so we encountered were visibly oiled. One, at Split Rock, was so badly smothered that I misidentified it as a Lesser Black-backed Gull.

Some five to ten per cent of them had black patches on their undersides. That is enough oil to kill and there is nothing one can do to try to catch them. Though some were flying irregularly they were all capable of being airborne and might still manage to scavenge in Cardiff. On their ledges, however, they preen themselves clean, and it is the ingested oil that is the killer – it rots their guts and in three days they are dead.

Steep Holm's problems were aired by Radio Bristol on the morning of 15 February 1991 in an interview with Roger Bennett, though he initially called the island "Lundy". Correcting him, I pointed out that "Lundy is the island with the bombs" – a reference to the emergency drop-zone for American B52 bombers returning from Iraq – "and we are the one with the oil".

I said that the oil slick was sloshing about backwards and forwards between Steep Holm and the Severn Bridge but that the tides were getting higher each night: "If the booms don't work then there is a real danger it will reach Slimbridge at 8.30 tonight."

Then I made some comparisons with the oil spills in the Persian Gulf: "Saddam's oil spill is international news – British Steel's doesn't even get into the London papers. Bird deaths here have been hugely underestimated – the majority have died at sea, probably quite quickly given the intense cold, and from past experience only a fraction of one per cent will be rescued. It's a unique oil spill because like the Gulf it's on a virtually landlocked piece of water, but it is also a tidal estuary."

Roger Bennett made the point that there was a great difference in scale. "The Bristol Channel has been designated as of international importance as a refuge for wildfowl and waders," I answered. "Ours will be a real disaster if the oil reaches either Slimbridge or Bridgwater Bay. We have probably lost half or more of our 200 Cormorants – the only ones in the Bristol Channel and the sister birds to those photographed in the harrowing shots of the Gulf spill.

"But we have had to rely mainly on boatmen's secondhand accounts via the Coastguard because we cannot even afford to be on the island out of season, let alone mount a highly specialised rescue operation. That's my challenge to British Steel – will they pay for us to see if we can salvage anything from this mess? It's due either to their accident or negligence, and either way the polluter must pay."

Seabird numbers are continuing to fall all around the British coasts. I cannot see any hope that the process can be put into reverse. For that to happen there would have to be no more pollution, no more accidents, a reduction in disturbance, and not too much adverse weather.

All that is just not going to happen so the coastal cliffs that once teemed with life are now largely a memory. Steep Holm has become a bird island that has only a few more birds than people see in their gardens at home. Even at the peak of the breeding season the general sound is no longer the raucous shrieks of gulls but the muted and melodious warbling of small birds in the bushes.

Following up the fate of those few birds that had been rescued from the oil spill I asked after the swan. "Oh," I was told. "The swan died."

WESTON & WORLE
News
The best one in Weston
'THE BEST ONE IN WESTON' / INCORPORATING 'THE ADVERTISER' / FREE TO 32,000 HOMES
THURSDAY, 21st FEBRUARY 1991

Don't miss next week's Weston & Worle News with full colour Homefinder

OPERATION CLEAN-UP

A MASSIVE clean-up operation has swung into action to rid Woodspring beaches of the oil slick.

Steep Holm bird colony may never recover

By Sam Block

Council workers have been scouring Weston beaches to remove every last trace of the oil which threatened the resort's famous sands.

The oil pollution which jeopardised the town's image as a clean and safe tourist resort has now been collected.

The operation did not begin until Friday because any cleaning up which began before would have been ruined by the rising tides washing up more oil.

Meanwhile experts fear the seabird population may not recover until the end of the century.

But for many birds it is too late – hundreds have

already died and many more have been covered by the heavy fuel oil which spilled out into the Bristol Channel last week.

Winter feeding grounds for rare wild fowl species have been hit including the bird colony at Steep Holm.

Rodney Legg, warden of Steep Holm feared the island's colony of birds may never be replaced. "The numbers will not recover until the end of the century and only then if there is no pollution or other damaging factors."

He said about 120 cormorants and 500 gulls were missing and some birds were so badly cov-

ered in oil he cannot recognise the species. Investigations are still underway to discover how the 20 tons of oil leaked

from a fractured pipe at the British Steel plant at Llanwern in South Wales. Woodspring hold British Steel fully responsible for the spill and still be seeking compensation to pay for the clean up.

The oil collected from the resort's beaches will now be shipped to the steel works in Wales and it will dispose of the fuel.

Spokesman for the National Rivers Authority Phil Hewett said a report had nearly been completed on the incident and legal advisors were considering whether or not to take action.

Walker & Ling

Yellow helicopter

"What colour's the yellow helicopter?" an excited Timothy Eden asked me when a Wessex came over as we went up the steps beside Garden Battery. "Why is it yellow?" he corrected himself, but it was too late for the embarrassed eight-year-old.

That was in 1986. The moment was recalled on 20 April 1991 when Royal Air Force Air-Sea Rescue helicopter 165, a yellow Wessex from Chivenor on the north Devon coast, came the length of the Bristol Channel to pick up Timmy; now known as Tim Wike since his mother's remarriage.

He had suffered a painful misadventure whilst exploring above Cliff Cottage. A boulder, about two hundredweight, had slid down between the sycamore trees and hit his foot. It was a serious injury but Timmy's damage could have been much worse. The island's emergency services could also have been less impressive.

Four things went right for us. Firstly, we knew of an area of radio silence, caused by the island topography, and took avoiding action on initially failing to raise the Coastguard. Secondly, we had a functioning air-strip, through the efforts of Tony Parsons at Easter in attempting to re-establish our patch of limestone grassland. Thirdly, the patient was strapped by Chris Maslen into the new Honda power carrier donated by Mrs Philippa Bowkett (against the manufacturer's warnings) and driven to the top of the island. Fourthly, the time for the entire operation – from the radio call-out which had the helicopter scrambled at Chivenor to its landing with Timmy a short distance from Cardiff Hospital – was 35 minutes. You would be hard pressed to better that with an emergency on the mainland, unless you were knocked over by a bus right outside the hospital.

Timmy had to have the dressing on his crushed big toe changed at hospital every day for a month and will have a long-term problem with his foot.

As for the offending stone, it has redeeming straight edges and it would be a waste to abandon it. Instead it will be built into a safety wall, at a point where parents have expressed concern about the drop to the under-cut shore below, and Timmy is determined to return and carve his initials in it.

The next chapter of accidents was on Friday 7 June 1991. Stephen Michell had taken over the captaincy of the *Waverley* paddle steamer for the season, from David Neill. Wind conditions were awkward when he arrived off the island and he parked her in the most sheltered spot, off the south-east corner below Tower Rock, to unload some 300 Bristol schoolchildren and about 50 adults from Penarth. They were decanted into the Weston ferry-boat *Silver Spray* in a shuttle service of runs across the remaining little bit of water to the shore.

Problems came after high water when the tide-race started to flow across the spot. It turned the *Waverley* into a spin and sent her alarmingly close to the rocks beside the beach. Stephen Michell started his engines and prepared to move to safety. Then he found his anchor was snagged.

He lifted it to water level but it was entangled in the island's pair of wartime undersea telephone cables. *Silver Spray* boatmen John Watts and Ashleigh Holtby used boat-hooks to prise them clear.

Later a girl fell into the sea. "A schoolgirl was swept into the sea and a birdwatcher injured on an incident-packed boat trip in the Bristol Channel," Andrew White would report in the Evening Post as he catalogued the troubles of the previous day. "The girl was hit by a big wave as she was boarding the pleasure craft *Silver Spray* at Steep Holm Island."

I did not see the incident but was told she was washed from the boarding plank by the sea. In fact she slipped off the plank as it moved in the waves. Anyway, she ended up in the water, and was pulled out by Ian Round and Mike Smith.

They had similar problems saving the boatmen's dinghy towards the end of the afternoon. White-water was surging up the beach and the last of the visitors were taken off the steps around the other side of Tower Rock at South Landing. Back on the beach, the dinghy was inundated as Ian Round and Mike Smith tied a line to it, from the *Silver Spray*. As the three of us waded in the waves to float it free, I literally put my foot in it – into a loop of the rescue rope beneath the turbid waters. It pulled tight but I was able to loosen it by pulling the dinghy towards me, and I jumped clear just in time as *Silver Spray* pulled it seawards. "Next time you have an annual meeting you can all sit there learning to tie knots!" John Watts jibed. Ian plaited the painter to show that he exempted knot training.

On the top of the island, ornithological twitcher Owen Taylor, aged 62, of Ash Hayes Road, Nailsea, had been injured in a scene which in Andrew White's words could have come straight from Alfred Hitchcock's classic thriller *The Birds*, and was left covered in blood when an irate gull swooped down and clawed him:

"I had just taken my cap off because the wind was so strong, when wallop! It hit me. I bled like the clappers. Whether it hit a vein or not I don't know. It was just one of those things."

The birds were particularly agitated because it was the height of the breeding season and the 500 or so pairs of gulls, many of them nesting beside the paths, had not experienced such a mass invasion of human beings for a couple of years. They were not used to having so many people about.

"They were going bananas," I admitted to Andrew White. "I was skimmed a few times and felt their feet through my hair. Quite a lot of people complained about the birds swooping low."

Earlier that week another party of visitors had startled one of the island's tiny Muntjac deer and sent it plunging over a cliff to its death. The lesson of both trips was that occasional mass influxes cause much more grief to wildlife than regular patterns of disturbance to which the birds and animals can adjust.

Yellow helicopter: Air-Sea Rescue flight 165, from RAF Chivenor, with Timothy Wike, suffering a crushed foot. He is being wheeled aboard, from the Honda power carrier, and would be in Cardiff hospital a few minutes later. Photographed by Rodney Legg on 20 April 1991.

'Cancelled': which brought his only smile of the day to retired gunner Cyril Stickland at 78, more than happy not to return to re-live wartime memories of emplacing 6-inch naval guns on Steep Holm in 1941. He called the island 'diabolical' and felt ill just looking at the choppy water. Seen from the east, on Knightstone Causeway. Photographed by Rodney Legg on 15 July 1991.

'Diabolical' memories

"Cancelled" is a common occurrence in the Steep Holm calendar. For 78-year-old wartime gunner Cyril Stickland, booked to return to the island for the unveiling of a commemorative stone at Garden Battery East on 15 July 1991, that word was music to his ears.

He "directed a hostile stare at the boats pitching violently on their moorings", Simon Pipe wrote next day in the Western Daily Press, and "the more he looked at that ugly brown sea, the more he wondered how they'd ever talked him into going back".

Then the boatmen decided that though they could deliver us to the island for our ceremony there was little chance they would be able to pick us up afterwards.

"It's a diabolical place," Cyril told press and radio reporters, as he waved my Sten-gun for the benefit of photographers. "We had no rations but dog biscuits and I spent my birthday out there eating hard-tack. For thirteen days it went on like that because the sea was too rough for the supply boat to land."

His most difficult task was winching four 6-inch naval guns from the beach to their emplacements on the top of the island. Most of the work had to be done at night, for fear of otherwise presenting the Luftwaffe with an irresistible target. "We couldn't have any light to work by, we daren't," he said.

Fortifying Steep Holm in 1941 was so indescribably awful that for Cyril the war could only get better. In comparison, he enjoyed the rest of his slog, via a bullet in his leg at Amiens, all the way to the Baltic and then across to Berlin. "The roughest time of all," he repeated without hesitation, his face visibly crumpling as he glanced out at Steep Holm in the middle of the cruel sea, "was over there!"

For us, the cancellation was the second disappointment of the day. The first was the non-appearance of Major David Benger, one of the last surviving staff officers of the Fixed Defences Severn, whose wife had been rushed into hospital for an emergency operation.

Simon Pipe also had a field day on that score: "Actually, admitted island Trust member Mrs Joan Rendell, Major Benger spent most of his time on the neighbouring island of Flat Holm, and never even set foot on Steep Holm."

David Benger would react strongly to this: "My Steep Holm pedigree is much better than has been reported. During the time we were at Barry, I made several trips to Steep Holm, to see the island, help plan the ultimate takeover, and to deliver pay to the troops already working out there. Finally, when Steep Holm was stood down, quite a number of 188 and 189 men [188 and 189 Coast Defence Batteries] were transferred to my Battery [146] on Flat Holm. So it would be a mistake to say that I never set foot on the island, though doubtless good copy for some frustrated journalist.''

As for Cyril Stickland, the report of his non-eventful day would be blighted by the fact that the newspaper consistently mis-spelt his surname as Strickland (sic).

So the Union Jack remained furled and the island's stone commemorating the fiftieth anniversary of the Second World War was left to unveil itself. The next wartime returnees who did manage to make it ashore on the island turned out to be German prisoners of war.

I should have invited them to perform the honour, particularly as the whole thing had been their show, but that seemed to be taking European togetherness a bit far.

THE ISLAND'S FOUR SECOND WORLD WAR SIX-INCH GUN BATTERIES WERE BUILT BY 930 PORT CONSTRUCTION AND REPAIR COMPANY OF THE ROYAL ENGINEERS AND THE PIONEER CORPS, FOR THE ROYAL ARTILLERY IN THE DEFENCE OF FREEDOM, JULY TO OCTOBER, 1941.
THIS STONE IS A MEMORIAL TO ALL WHO SERVED ON STEEP HOLM AND IN THE FIXED DEFENCES (SEVERN). IT WAS UNVEILED ON THE OCCASION OF THE FIFTIETH ANNIVERSARY OF THE ISLAND'S FORTIFICATION.

MAJOR DAVID BENGER,
O/C 146 COAST BATTERY, R.A.
RODNEY LEGG, WARDEN, STEEP HOLM ISLAND.

Words in stone: for those who served in the Fixed Defences (Severn). On the side of the 1941-built gun emplacement at Garden Battery East. Seen from the north-west. Photographed by Rodney Legg in 1991.

144

Masons: Ian White (right) and Terry Hack, receiving a helping hand, as they install a stone at Garden Battery East to commemorate those who served on the island and in the Bristol Channel, for 'the fiftieth anniversary of the island's fortification'. In 1941 the Royal Engineers displaced a Victorian gun barrel (right) into the foreground. Seen from the west. Photographed by Rodney Legg in 1991.

German PoWs: Hans Messmer (left) and Max Flemming return to Steep Holm where they were prisoner of war, dismantling fortifications in 1946. Seen outside the Barracks, beside the 24-pounder George III cannon, from the south. Photographed by Rodney Legg in 1991.

Return of the German PoWs

Two German prisoners of war returned to Steep Holm on 17 August 1991 to relive wartime memories. They had spent the summer of 1946 dismantling military installations after the Royal Artillery vacated the island.

"There were twenty-five of us, with one British sergeant as our guard," said Max Flemming, born in 1923 and from Dresden, who now lives in Stourport-on-Severn, Worcestershire. An Unterofficier in the élite Hermann Göring tank division, he had been captured by the 52nd (Highland) Division on 22 October 1944, during the Battle of Arnhem.

That day and the Steep Holm summer were both remembered in sharp focus.

"We camped here, in this row of three Nissen huts, and the latrines were at that end," he told me, as we stood in a cutting behind Split Rock Battery. "This was where we had our stove, on these bricks."

I said the remains of the cast-iron tortoise stove were still in place when the Kenneth Allsop Memorial Trust took over the island as a nature reserve and started clearing the remainder of the wartime debris: "Had I realised you were coming back I would have kept the top of it to give you as a souvenir!"

Then I ventured to inform the Germans that the Trust had been less than impressed by the effort put into the post-war clearance.

"I must admit we didn't work ourselves to death," Max replied. "We had a really cushy number here and the sergeant couldn't have cared less. He had only his last year to do. There was an engineer who came across on the launch from Barry with our supplies and he set the next assignment.

"But he would only turn up once every two or three weeks and a couple of days later we'd done what he wanted and the rest of the time was our own. The chaps from Barry were more interested in giving us lists of piping, tap and sanitary fittings that they'd sell on the black market, for high prices because production of all that sort of thing had been stopped by the war."

"The highlight was the seagull breeding season. We had a wonderful time eating gull eggs and the young birds as well. They were delicious. It wasn't that we didn't have enough rations, it was just an adventure we got up to."

Hans Messmer, born in 1924, was revisiting the island from Sürth, a village near Köln. He recalled the night when a large vessel was nearly shipwrecked on the rocks. A lad from one of the huts reported seeing lights through the driving rain. Hans, who had been a signals operator in the German Navy up to the surrender of the Cherbourg peninsula, was the only person on the island who could relay messages in morse code. The ship flashed that its engines had broken down and that it was drifting helplessly in the heavy seas.

The sergeant used the island's underwater telephone link to the mainland to contact Barry for a lifeboat.

"Boat coming," Hans signalled using a Tilley-lamp, and the thankful captain later visited the island with a letter of commendation and to give his personal thanks.

"It was a nice touch," Max remarked. "Troubles were over."

Their biggest task on the island was the removal of a jetty of steel girders that had been constructed on the pebble beach by the Royal Engineers in 1941. The lower bolts, which had been underwater for most of the time, could still be undone, but those above the tide-line were badly corroded and had to be flame-cut.

"There was a crane that had to be taken off," Max recalled, "as well as the timbers. We also removed winches that had been used with the railway. As for the guns that were on the island, those had gone before we arrived."

For me, the disappointment was that all this information had come too late for my newly published book on *Steep Holm at War*. That's always the way.

When he returned home, Max Flemming compounded my grief by writing with another batch of reminiscences: "You might be interested to know that the so-called escape attempt by two PoWs did not take place from Flat Holm" – as recorded by amateur historians of the Severn Sea – "but from Steep Holm. The truth behind this adventure was an attempt to fetch cigarettes from the lighthouse men [on Flat Holm] for our two guards.

"A sudden storm caught our lads half way across and they drifted out into the mouth of the channel only to be rescued, half-drowned, by the then lightship.

"The press misinterpreted the whole story. What was not known to them was the fact that we had cut the telephone wire to the mainland to protect our British guards from punishment for not reporting this event. However, to no avail, but I can't remember what happened to them.

"I'm telling you all this so you can put the true story to your fellow members, as I was wrong myself in assuming it took place from Flat Holm. Hans has put me right on this; it was a long time ago and memories fade."

Then, with unintentional irony – given that he was partially responsible for the demolition of our wartime jetty – Herr Flemming raised a recurrent latter-day problem: "May I suggest investigating better landing facilities on Steep Holm?"

Rebuilding: Chris Maslen (centre) laying concrete with Woodspring District Council chief executive Bob Moon (left), and boatman John Watts (right) propping up the cliff. Seen from the north. Photographed by Rodney Legg in April 1990.

Frank Watts's heroic rescue

Publication of *Steep Holm at War* prompted Mrs Mary Sandover to recall her associations with the island: "I thought you might be interested in the enclosed cutting from the News Chronicle dated 2 February 1940."

"Fishermen Risk Death to bring Coastguard to Hospital," read the banner heading.

"I happen to be the daughter of the said coastguard," Mrs Sandover wrote from 42 Kinghill Gardens, Nailsea. What amazed me was that the principal hero of the story was boatman Frank Watts, the father of the present Frank Watts who continues to own and operate the series of vessels that have been chartered by the Allsop Trust.

How "the well-known Weston brothers, Frank and Ted Watts" rescued one of the coastguards stationed on Steep Holm is told in graphic detail:

"When they paid a visit to a lonely Bristol Channel island yesterday [31 January 1940] they learned of the plight of one of the coastguards." Harry Spencer Phillips, aged 58, of Rhydyblewyn Road, Cyncoed, Cardiff, was suffering from double pneumonia. A merchant navy captain, he had served in the Royal Naval Reserve in the Great War, with the rank of Lieutenant-Commander.

"An attempt to take him off then, using a door as a stretcher, proved impracticable owing to the treacherous condition of the narrow rocky passage down the cliffs.

"Mr Frank Watts reported the circumstances to Weston ambulance headquarters today [1 February], and a special collapsible stretcher was procured. Four ambulance men accompanied the Watts brothers out to sea in a small motor-boat in unfavourable weather conditions, and despite the difficulty of finding a solid foothold they managed to bring the sick man down the 200 feet cliffs to the waterside.

"Even then their troubles were not over, for fierce currents and rolling swell threatened to wash the boat on to the rocks every time it neared the stretcher party.

"Eventually magnificent seamanship by Frank Watts worked it close enough for the ambulance men to seize a chance and the stretcher was safely shipped. Wrapped in innumerable blankets the sick man was landed at Weston and taken to hospital."

Asked by a reporter how it had been "out there", Frank made a typically stoical remark of the sort his son would be producing as other adventures came into question over the next half century: "It was just a job of work, and we did not expect it to be easy."

It would be ever thus. For the same post brought the Taunton RSPB Members' Group Newsletter for November 1991 with an article by Mary Pointing on a visit to Steep Holm that took place on 1 June 1991. Despite the "tiny wavelets gently lapping at the slipway," at Weston, there was talk of it being a very different story "out there". Because the wind was north-easterly, "there was doubt (a) whether we could land at the normal landing place, or (b) whether we could land at all. We must get there and see."

The wind freshened and Mary and her friend, Sheila, experienced an uncomfortable hour's crossing with water slapping over the side as "we see-sawed our way through the fast-running tide", only to find after "bobbing steadily onward" that there was no hope of beaching at the usual landing place. Instead they came in at the remains of the emergency South Landing, where I was awaiting their arrival: "One of the Trust personnel already on the island had come down on to the black rocks at the base of the cliff and was waiting to help us land. The boat was manoeuvred nearer inshore (a process which took ten or more heaving minutes) and he caught the rope thrown to him from the boat and we all scrambled out as best we could."

By four o'clock in the afternoon the situation had not changed and the weary party "scrambled, slid, hopped and jumped down the track to the rocks" at South Landing. Once again *Silver Spray* was persuaded into its tight corner, put there by John Watts's ever brilliant seamanship and held by Ashleigh Holtby managing to look suave and casual at the end of a boathook.

I was herding the visitors from the rear, with my own handful in the form of tabby cat Salman Legg who is the first to jump ashore on arrival, but thinks we are mad to throw ourselves into the sea in misguided attempts at abandoning the island.

This time neither Salman nor I had any problem with the "rickety narrow plank" which is the lifeline between the shore and the boat. On the water, however, it was another matter, as Mary Pointing describes: "All aboard (including one of the Trust members with the island cat!) we set forth into the current once more. If the journey over was a bit bumpy, then the return was a roller-coaster, with hissing water spilling frequently over the side, and soaking the family which had the misfortune to be sitting there. The cat, which had been remarkably calm until we were out at sea, took fright, and shot under the cabin seat, where it cowered in trauma for the rest of the journey. I think we were all glad when we at last landed at Anchor Head and climbed unsteadily out on to the tide-washed muddy slipway."

Yet, there had been perfect crossings, even for Salman, in the summer of 1991. To prove the point, I tried to put a date on the trip when another Taunton birdwatcher, 13-year-old James McGill from Cresswell Avenue, Staplegrove, visited the island with his grandfather, retired police marksman William McGill.

I photographed them in the stern of the boat on the return trip, which was memorable as this was a warm and precious idyllic evening with a flat sea and the sun setting across Bridgwater Bay.

It must have existed, but instead the diary recorded adverse events, with the word "Cancelled" being commonplace. Sometimes a reason had been scrawled in. The first failure of the year was a warning that these days weather predictions are not to be discounted, even when they appear to be completely wrong.

Such was the case on Saturday 6 April: "Still, clear morning but winds 'with squalls of 70 mph' forecast for the West this afternoon."

The morning remained suitable for boating. Then came the promised gusts, spot on time at my high-sided workplace in Wincanton, which is thirty miles inland. They lifted off three slates.

Had we ignored the warnings and gone to sea we would have been staying on the island.

Similar conditions did not prevent *Silver Spray* from venturing "out there" to pick up Crewkerne ornithologist Tony Parsons from his week of bird-ringing in September 1991. Until that moment his principal excitements had been the netting of a Treecreeper – "first one I've seen on the island although there's at least one recorded from the 1960s" – and the capture of 25-plus new insect species for the island.

An horrendous rescue would cap it all: "The pick-up on the Saturday was the worst I've ever seen from the island – I was extremely glad that there was no one with me! John did extremely well to keep the boat in one piece and the right way up."

Paradise: birdwatcher James McGill, at age 13, with grandfather William McGill, a retired police marksman, homeward bound from Steep Holm after an idyllic day. They are in the stern of *Silver Spray* and the sun begins to sink over Bridgwater Bay. Seen from the south-east. Photographed by Rodney Legg in 1991.

12 — EVENING POST, TUESDAY, FEBRUARY 19, 1991

'Ghost' island fear

POST FOCUS ON SEA BIRDS IN OIL DISASTER

Steep Holm Island: wildlife hit by oil slick

Story: John Thompson
Pictures: Nigel Tailby

HORROR stretched across warden Rodney Legg's face as he discovered a large proportion of Steep Holm's cormorant population had been wiped out by the Bristol Channel oil slick.

The Evening Post joined him on his return to the island to check the effects of the latest ecological disaster to hit the wildlife sanctuary's sea bird population.

Last week, an estimated 6,000 gallons of oil leaked from a fractured pipe at the Llanwern steelworks, near Newport, to form an ugly slick in the already murky channel waters.

Eerie

His greatest worry is that Steep Holm will degenerate into a 50 acre ghost island. A wildlife sanctuary without any sea birds.

Mr Legg believed the cormorants would be among the species to suffer most because they need to dive deep below the waves to feed on fish and other marine life. As our boat nosed towards their breeding ground

Devastated: The depleted cormorant population

on the steep craggy north face, his fears proved right.

"Look at that — there are usually between 20 and 30 perched on that corner and all I can see is one," he said.

There was an eerie silence as our eyes scanned upwards when the boat turned and moved along the high stretch of rock. "The most I can see is 40," someone shouted and we all agreed.

"Late last year that face was covered in a mass of cormorants, totalling 200 or more. It is the only colony in the Bristol Channel and it has been

Grim search: An inflatable boat crew looks for oiled birds

practically destroyed," said Mr Legg.

There were also signs that numbers were well down on the island's gull population. "Look at that bird over there, it's so badly covered in oil, I cannot recognise the species," he said.

We scrambled ashore and across oil-covered seaweed and debris for a closer investigation with Clevedon coastguard Brian Chislett, a Steep Holm Trust member. The black plumaged cormorants looked stunned.

The widows and widowers among them will not have

enough time to pair-up and get together for breeding this year," said Mr Legg.

As the boat returned to Weston-super-Mare Mr Legg said: "This is the second major disaster to strike the island in recent years. Our herring gull population has dropped dramatically from peak proportions of 10,000 in the early 1970s to 100 pairs at the moment. This has been caused by avian botulism, a food poison picked up when the bird's scavenge on rubbish tips in the region.

Balancing act: island warden Rodney Legg walking on walls, all the more precarious in that he built them. Seen at the Inn, from the east. Photographed by John Pitfield in 1990.

Big boat: *Balmoral* moored off the Barracks and Jon Davies at 12, visiting the island. He is the son of her first-mate, Ted Davies. Seen from the north. Photographed by Rodney Legg on 29 July 1991.

In step: the Honda carrier given to the island by Mrs Philippa Bowkett, which soon went on to do other things at Chris Maslen's behest, also prohibited by the manufacturer's handbook. Seen using its tank-tracks to climb the beach-steps, from the east. Photographed by Rodney Legg in 1991.

OPPOSITE:
Arrival: the power carrier donated by Mrs Philippa Bowkett making landfall from *Silver Spray* with Terry Gore and Ian Round helping to manoeuvre it from below and Ashleigh Holtby and Chris Maslen steering from above. Paul Stone watches from the right (standing at the edge). Seen from the west. Photographed by Rodney Legg in 1991.

The Tornado crash

Shortly after the Gulf War, a Royal Air Force Panavia Tornado GR.1, from Marham, Norfolk, crashed into the Bristol Channel – only a mile south of the Barracks on Steep Holm – on 12 September 1991. The pilot reported an engine fire and Swansea coastguards heard him say: "We are ejecting."

The fighter was then heading south from the Monkstone Rock. Both crewmen were recovered, almost unhurt, from dinghies in the vicinity of Flat Holm. One rescue was carried out by a helicopter from RAF Chivenor and the other by the lifeboat from Barry Dock.

As for the aircraft, it continued pilotless for five miles, passing beside Flat Holm and then screeching over the middle of Steep Holm at not much more than the island's height, 256 feet.

Derek Payne saw it trailing smoke as it plunged into the sea. The Tornado probably came down on a bed of Holm sand and could well have been broken up by the tides. A few days later a search vessel arrived on the scene and proceeded to trawl electronic detection gear backwards and forwards across the northern part of Bridgwater Bay for three weeks, without any apparent result.

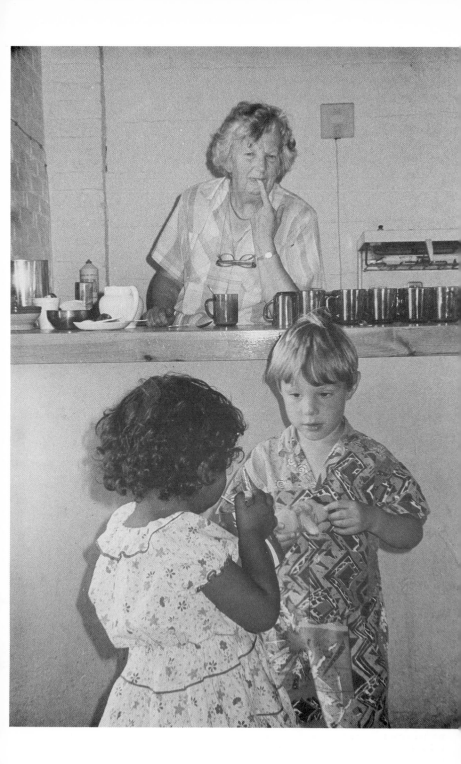

Alcohol sales banned

One of the island's unusual operational difficulties slipped into the public domain on 13 September 1991 when Chris Rundle reported in the Western Daily Press that time had been called on "one of the West's offshore drinking dens". The executive council of the Kenneth Allsop Memorial Trust was closing the bar in the Barracks.

It had functioned for ten years without a licence. Lundy Island, Sir John Smith has told me, also operates its public house without one. In neither case have the licensing authorities requested an application.

Chris Rundle gave a different reason for the closure: "The end has come after a spate of thefts from the bar's stockroom, all, it seems, the work of someone with a taste for bottles of ready-mixed whisky and dry ginger. A case of bottles has been drained this summer but the culprit has not been traced."

I was quoted as saying: "We have decided it is better not to run a bar at all. It's a shame, but if the visitors want a drink in future they'll have to bring it with them."

Some members of the Allsop Trust were less than impressed by this logic. "It's like closing the railways because you cannot make the trains run on time," said one stalwart.

Put accountants in charge and you'll see even more perversity, like their advice to the North Sea ferry company that was losing money on transportation but making profits out of duty-free sales. "Close the ferries and concentrate on the duty-free shops," accountants suggested.

At least, as the rebuilding edges towards roof height, it will save me from demands that the resurrected former Inn beside the beach should once more be licensed premises.

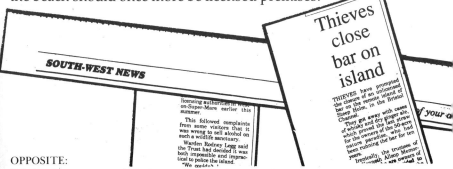

SOUTH-WEST NEWS

licensing authorities in Weston-Super-Mare earlier this summer.

This followed complaints from some visitors that it was wrong to sell alcohol on such a wildlife sanctuary.

Warden Rodney Legg said the Trust had decided it was both impossible and impractical to police the island.

"We could...

Thieves close bar on island

THIEVES have prompted the closure of an unlicensed bar on the remote island of Steep Holm, in the Bristol Channel.

They got away with cases of whisky and dry ginger ale, which proved the last straw for the owners of the 50-acre nature paradise, who had been running the bar for ten years.

Ironically, the trustees of the Kenneth Allsop Memorial are owners of

OPPOSITE:
Ethnic mix: young people in the snack-bar in the Barracks on Steep Holm. Contemplative tea-person is Mrs Philippa Bowkett, from Brean on the Somerset shore, perhaps considering her next bout of fund-raising for the island's good causes. The brick-wall of the counter held a stage, built in 1941-42 for ENSA performances when the building was the wartime Naafi. Seen from the east. Photographed by Rodney Legg in 1991.

'Up mitha fludde'

On that point, one of life's endless inherent contradictions, I'll suspend the story of Allsop Island and content myself with a single observation concerning human behaviour. When waiting for the boat to take them home, the males of the species invariably sit on the beach and throw stones in a seaward direction. I hope the wildlife appreciates that such cacophonic echoes from the eastern cliffs generally herald the imminent departure of mankind.

There will be other Steep Holm adventures for the new millennium. Meanwhile, until you can walk there in the next Ice Age – stumbling over the remains of the Severn Barrage – there are just two facts to remember.

The best tidal prospects for an island crossing are to sail either 90 minutes before or after high-water. The latter gives the optimum chance for a day trip because you can then return with the evening tide.

As the Wadden Sea inhabitants put it in their ancient Frisian toast – "uth mitha ebbe, up mitha fludde".

"Wadden" is the Dutch for tidal-flats, and theirs are the widest in Europe. It is a saying which Weston-super-Mare boatman John ('Kenny') Watts used with us, though in Anglo-Australian translation – "out with the ebb, up with the flood".